PROVIDENCE

The Silent Sovereignty of God

PROVIDENCE

The Silent Sovereignty of God

CECIL MAY JR.

GOSPEL
ADVOCATE
A TRUSTED NAME SINCE 1855

Also by Cecil May Jr.
Bible Questions and Answers

Published by Gospel Advocate Co.
1006 Elm Hill Pike, Nashville, TN 37210
www.gospeladvocate.com

ISBN: 978-0-89225-649-5

DEDICATION

To Winnie Williamson May, my wife and the mother of my children. By the providence of God, "perhaps," she made contact with me in her search for truth regarding Christ, salvation and the Lord's church. She readily accepted the truths presented to her in Scripture. In two weeks, she was baptized into Christ; in two months, we were engaged. For 60 years, as of April 15, 2014, she has been my wife, my companion and my helper, "the wind beneath my wings." Whatever good I may have accomplished would not have been possible without her counsel and encouragement.

The mighty God, Omniscient One!
His ways we cannot trace.
He reckons ev'ry good begun
And crowns it with His grace.

Lo! I can see Him in His word –
I will not doubt or fear;
My steps are ordered of the Lord,
His guiding hand is near.

No trial can my spirit break,
For God will not forsake;
He will with each temptation make
A way for my escape.

The future beckons and I bow –
My God removes the care!
Behold, He goes before me now,
And will my way prepare.

He's here, and there, and ev'rywhere
In all the ways I've trod.
I've never passed beyond the sphere
Of the providence of God.

– "The Providence of God"
L.O. Sanderson, 1965

Table of
CONTENTS

Foreword

For years, Cecil May Jr. has answered serious Bible questions for readers of the *Magnolia Messenger*, and in more recent years, he has penned a column in the *Gospel Advocate*. His gracious style and wisdom have endeared him to his readers and caused his wise answers to be classics. Although a scholar in his own right, Cecil has never forgotten the serious student in the pew. He has that rare ability to explain complicated issues in simple terms.

Heroes come in many forms, but my heroes have always been preachers. I look for scholarly men who love the Lord, hold the Bible in the highest esteem and study it continually, show balance and common sense in their approach to issues and problems, and treat others with care and respect. Cecil is such a man, and I have regarded him as one of my heroes and friends for many years.

When Cecil tackles a topic, he does more than look at the surface issues. He helps the reader understand underlying assumptions, the importance of the questions, and the significance of the answers. Cecil does his homework before he speaks; he does not shoot from the hip. His exhaustive knowledge of Scripture and his broad understanding of current thought have helped him to understand not only what is being asked but also why.

Cecil understands God has not revealed everything to us (Deuteronomy 29:29); for this reason, he is unafraid to say that we may never know some things. Cecil, as a wise student of Scripture, says all that God says on a matter and hushes when God hushes. He is not so presumptuous as to speak with certainty when God has left us with a "perhaps" (Esther 4:13-14; Philemon 15-16).

Cecil believes in a God who provides for His people, and this book on providence is certainly a gift to those who want to know more about the special providence of God. We serve a God who invites us to ask, to seek and to knock, knowing we have a Father who will not serve us a stone for bread or a serpent for fish (Matthew 7:7-11).

More than 30 years ago, I took a course in eschatology (the study of last things) under Cecil at the church building in Senatobia, Miss. Cecil also preached a gospel meeting for us during that time. I learned to value his knowledge and have kept his notes to this day.

Reading this book, I treasured each chapter and felt I was once again Cecil's student. Although I took a course on providence and suffering many years ago in graduate school, I have learned much from this book about God's special dealings with His children. Every reader will learn much as well and will grow to love God more for all He does for us.

Everyone who loves the Lord will benefit greatly from this timely and interesting study into the special providence of God. Each one will come away with a renewed appreciation for what God has done for us.

– Phil Sanders, Speaker
In Search of the Lord's Way
Edmond, Okla.

Preface

I n September 2009, the Eastern Meadows Church of Christ in Montgomery, Ala., invited me to present a four-lesson series on the providence of God. Although I strongly believed in providence and had often referred to it in lessons, I had never studied or addressed it comprehensively. Later, when I was asked to present the same lessons at several other congregations, it became evident there was a hunger for teaching on this subject and for the encouragement the biblical promises related to providence bring to the children of God.

The word "providence" appears only once in the King James Version (Acts 24:2). When the Jewish rulers were accusing Paul before the Roman governor Felix, an orator named Tertullus presented their case. Tertullus began with customary praise for the governor: "Seeing that by thee we enjoy great quietness, and that very worthy deeds are done unto this nation by thy providence, We accept it always, and in all places, most noble Felix, with all thankfulness" (vv. 2-3). "Providence" in that instance has the same sense it has when we speak of the providence of God. Newer versions usually translate the word "foresight," although the New American Standard Bible also uses "providence." The same Greek word is translated "provision" by the King James Version in Romans: "But put ye on the Lord Jesus Christ, and make no provision for the flesh, to fulfil the lusts thereof" (13:14).

Literature about God's providence distinguishes between "general providence" and "special providence." General providence refers to God's continued care for His entire creation. Moses, Jesus and Paul all spoke of it: "Behold, to the LORD your God belong heaven and the heaven of heavens, the earth with all that is in it" (Deuteronomy 10:14). "For he makes his sun rise on the evil and on the good, and sends rain on the just and on the unjust" (Matthew 5:45).

> The God who made the world and everything in it, being Lord of heaven and earth, does not live in temples made by man, nor is he served by human hands, as though he needed anything, since he himself gives to all mankind life and breath and everything. And he made from one man every nation of mankind to live on all the face of the earth, having determined allotted periods and the boundaries of their dwelling place, that they should seek God, and perhaps feel their way toward him and find him. Yet he is actually not far from each one of us, for "In him we live and move and have our being"; as even some of your own poets have said, "For we are indeed his offspring." (Acts 17:24-28)

Special providence, on the other hand, is that particular care God exercises toward His faithful children. Special providence is the concern of this book. Although the phrase "providence of God" is not found in Scripture, the Bible is permeated with the concept. "In all your ways acknowledge him, and he will make straight your paths" (Proverbs 3:6). The psalmist added, "The steps of a man are established by the LORD, when he delights in his way" (Psalm 37:23). Nehemiah recounted the history of God's dealings with Israel, beginning with the creation of the world. He continued through the promises made to Abraham, the leadership of Moses in the wilderness, the conquest of Canaan, and the exile in Babylon – all the way to the Israelites' return to their land, though they were still an enslaved people (Nehemiah 9). Through it all, Nehemiah saw the providential hand of God preserving the Israelites as a people for the accomplishment of God's promises.

> And you warned them in order to turn them back to your law. Yet they acted presumptuously and did not obey your commandments, but sinned against your rules, which if a person does them, he shall live by them, and they turned a stubborn shoulder and stiffened their neck and would not obey. Many years you bore with them and warned them by your Spirit through your prophets. Yet they would not give ear. Therefore you gave them into the hand of the peoples of the lands. Nevertheless, in your great mercies you did not

make an end of them or forsake them, for you are a gracious
and merciful God. (vv. 29-31)

God's special providence aided the patriarchs and extends from them
to us. The writer of Hebrews reminded us, "And all these, though
commended through their faith, did not receive what was promised,
since God had provided something better for us, that apart from us
they should not be made perfect" (Hebrews 11:39-40).

The reader is invited to follow along as we explore this biblical doctrine as it applies to God's faithful children today. Realizing that God
has not retired but is still working to bless His people encourages us
in service to Him and to others, knowing that in the Lord our labor
is not in vain.

1

What Is
PROVIDENCE?

Deism is the view that God created the world in the beginning but, like a clockmaker, set it to the correct time and left it running without any further attention or intervention. Some Christians, who fail to recognize the difference between the signs and wonders God used to confirm the validity of His human messengers in Bible times and how God works today, deny any divine activity taking place in today's world, equating any intervention by God with miraculous activity.

Yet the concept of providence presumes that God is still at work in the world He created. "Provide" is at the root of the word "providence." God does provide good things for His people, and His loving care is always behind His every action on our behalf. We are to cast all our anxieties on God because He cares for us (1 Peter 5:7).

God Keeps His Promises

Scripture makes several promises to God's faithful that, if true, require that God is still at work on behalf of His children today. They include the following:

- "But seek first the kingdom of God and his righteousness, and all these things will be added to you" (Matthew 6:33).

- "Are not two sparrows sold for a penny? And not one of them will fall to the ground apart from your Father. But even the hairs of your head are all numbered. Fear not, therefore; you are of more value than many sparrows" (Matthew 10:29-31).

- "And we know that for those who love God all things work together for good, for those who are called according to his purpose" (Romans 8:28).

- "No temptation has overtaken you that is not common to man. God is faithful, and he will not let you be tempted beyond your ability, but with the temptation he will also provide the way of escape, that you may be able to endure it" (1 Corinthians 10:13).

- "Keep your life free from love of money, and be content with what you have, for he has said, 'I will never leave you nor forsake you.' So we can confidently say, 'The Lord is my helper; I will not fear; what can man do to me?' " (Hebrews 13:5-6).

If God does not affect anything currently occurring in the world, these promises are all meaningless or false. Some will ask, then, "If God turns calamities into assets, provides a way of escape to accompany every temptation, and is always protectively with us, how is that different from miracles?" The answer lies in the nature and purpose of biblical miracles.

The Miracles of God

The term "miracle" is used very loosely in common conversation today to refer to any wonderful thing from childbirth to surviving an accident that produced severe injuries. That leads to an unfortunate misunderstanding, for when we say, as the Bible teaches, that God is not working miracles today, we are often understood to be saying

God does not do any wonderful things today. That is clearly false and not at all what is meant.

John's favorite word for miracle in his gospel was "sign." Biblical miracles were events that could not have occurred naturally: a withered arm immediately restored, a man born blind given immediate sight, a dead person raised. John's word "sign" reminds us that miracles had significance. They signified something. Specifically, they demonstrated conclusively that the person working the miracle had the approval of God in what he said and taught.

Nicodemus, a ruler of the Jews, recognized the significance of the miracles of Jesus. He said, "Rabbi, we know that you are a teacher come from God, for no one can do these signs that you do unless God is with him" (John 3:2). After recording Jesus' resurrection to demonstrate that Jesus was the promised Anointed One of God, John wrote: "Now Jesus did many other signs in the presence of the disciples, which are not written in this book; but these are written so that you may believe that Jesus is the Christ, the Son of God, and that by believing you may have life in his name" (20:30-31).

It limits God, however, to say that if He works, it can only be through a miracle.

Providence Beyond Miracles

Part of the penalty King David faced, as predicted by Nathan the prophet, because he had Uriah killed "with the sword of the Ammonites" and had taken Uriah's wife, Bathsheba, to be his wife was that "the sword [would] never depart from [his] house" (2 Samuel 12:9-10). Partially fulfilling that curse, David's son Absalom rebelled against him, raising a sizable army and forcing David to flee Jerusalem. David was particularly disheartened by the news that his most trusted counselor, Ahithophel, had joined Absalom's rebellion. "Now in those days the counsel that Ahithophel gave was as if one consulted the word of God; so was all the counsel of Ahithophel esteemed, both by David and by Absalom" (16:23).

When David was told "Ahithophel is among the conspirators with Absalom," he prayed, "O LORD, please turn the counsel of Ahithophel into foolishness" (2 Samuel 15:31). God did not answer David's prayer by confounding Ahithophel's mind and making him give bad advice. On the contrary, if Absalom had followed Ahithophel's counsel, he likely would have won the kingdom. However, Absalom had another counselor, Hushai the Archite, who gave opposite counsel. "And Absalom and all the men of Israel said, 'The counsel of Hushai the Archite is better than the counsel of Ahithophel' " (17:14), and they rejected Ahithophel's advice.

We would not know just from the recorded events that the Lord was in anyway involved and was answering David's prayer. There was no miracle. It is not at all out of the ordinary for a hotheaded young man to reject wise counsel. Absalom did and was ultimately defeated, but not without the help of God's providence. We know this because Scripture says so: "For the LORD had ordained to defeat the good counsel of Ahithophel, so that the LORD might bring harm upon Absalom" (2 Samuel 17:14).

Through a favorable set of experiences that resulted in my knowing and being known by most of the churches of Christ in Mississippi and my having had academic teaching and administrative experience, I became president of Magnolia Bible College. I believed, as did several others associated with MBC, that the providence of God had worked to prepare me for that task and bring me there. The work at Magnolia went very well, but there was more than a little opposition from outside the college based on misrepresentations and untruths. Time and resources needed elsewhere were spent refuting the erroneous charges.

What we could not do, however – and here is the point of this recital of history – is say: "God has placed me here providentially. He would not have prepared me for this in the way He has unless He approved this work. Fighting Magnolia Bible College is therefore fighting against God." Providence cannot be as certainly known to be God's work as is restoring a withered arm. Providence, therefore, cannot be a sign of God's approval as is raising someone from the dead. Miracles are a "sign" of God's endorsement. God's providential working is not obvious enough to serve as such a sign.

God Is Always Good

God's providential care does not always work in ways we think best. Sometimes circumstances we might never think of as providential may actually serve a providential purpose.

A faithful Christian has an automobile wreck; his car is totaled, but he comes out unscathed. "The Lord was with him," it is said; "God is good." And it is true that God is good. But if a faithful Christian has a wreck and is crippled for life or is killed, it is still true: "The Lord was with him; God is good." For the faithful child of God, that is always true.

Faithful Christians serve together on a battlefield in Afghanistan. They are prayed for fervently by their families and fellow Christians back home. One comes home safely; another does not. In His providence, God was with both. God is always good.

How do we know with whom the Lord rides? According to a story sometimes told, a preacher was traveling along a mountain road and came up behind a man driving very erratically. The preacher followed him for a while, worried the man might cause a serious wreck. Finally, he decided to pass him.

Just as he did so, the man swerved toward him. The only way for the preacher to prevent a wreck was to wrench the steering wheel violently, and when he did, he went careening off the mountainside. The erratic driver stopped his car and stumbled down the hill, obviously intoxicated, in time to see the preacher crawl out of his wrecked car.

"Are you all right?" he asked.

"Yes," the preacher gratefully said, "the Lord was with me."

"Well," the drunk said, "next time you better let Him ride with me. You're gonna get Him killed!"

God is always good, but we may not always understand His ways. On an occasion a number of years ago, God was with a faithful gospel preacher's godly grandson and his Christian family when the grandson died; God is good. God was with Shadrach, Meshach and Abednego, saving them in the fiery furnace; God is good. God was with Job as he scratched his sores with a broken piece of pottery in the midst of his sudden poverty and loss of all he had; God is good.

The writer of Hebrews named a number of individuals and the great things they accomplished by obedient faith (Hebrews 11). Then he added some others without specifying their victories:

> And what more shall I say? For time would fail me to tell of Gideon, Barak, Samson, Jephthah, of David and Samuel and the prophets – who through faith conquered kingdoms, enforced justice, obtained promises, stopped the mouths of lions, quenched the power of fire, escaped the edge of the sword, were made strong out of weakness, became mighty in war, put foreign armies to flight. Women received back their dead by resurrection. (vv. 32-35)

Obviously, God was with each of them; God is good.

Sometimes, however, we forget about "others." The Hebrews writer did not.

> Some were tortured, refusing to accept release, so that they might rise again to a better life. Others suffered mocking and flogging, and even chains and imprisonment. They were stoned, they were sawn in two, they were killed with the sword. They went about in skins of sheep and goats, destitute, afflicted, mistreated – of whom the world was not worthy – wandering about in deserts and mountains, and in dens and caves of the earth. (Hebrews 11:35-38)

Make no mistake; God was with them, too. The writer said, "And all these, though commended through their faith, did not receive what was promised, since God had provided something better for us, that apart from us they should not be made perfect" (Hebrews 11:39-40). Even in death, torture and seeming defeat, God was providing and blessing. Some providential actions of God are not apparent until the after-life.

The truth is as stated by three Hebrew young men when Nebuchadnezzar was about to throw them into an overheated furnace: "If this be so, our God whom we serve is able to deliver us from the burning fiery furnace, and he will deliver us out of your hand, O king. But if not, be it known to you, O king, that we will not serve your gods or worship the golden image that you have set up" (Daniel 3:17-18). Likewise, we can confidently say: "Our God whom we serve is able. But if not, by the providence of God, we will be victors either way."

Questions

1. Is "providence" a Bible word?

2. What is the difference between "general providence" and "special providence"?

3. What are some of God's promises that necessarily imply His providential activity in the world today?

4. How does the story of David, Absalom and Ahithophel illustrate the difference between providential and miraculous activity?

5. How might God's providence be at work when a faithful Christian dies in an accident?

6. When we do not understand God's providence, what can we always know?

7. The Hebrews writer told of many who accomplished great things and enjoyed wonderful victories by faith (Hebrews 11). How do those in verses 35-38 illustrate God's providence?

8. God miraculously rescued Shadrach, Meshach and Abednego from the fiery furnace. Did they consider the possibility that He might not choose to do so?

For Discussion

1. If God's providential activity actually does change outcomes, how is that different from performing miracles?

2. What is deism? Does the Bible confirm or deny this view?

3. When something good happens, Christians often say, "God is good." How can Christians know that God is always good, even when something bad happens?

PROVIDENCE
Is "Perhaps"

"Glad to see you. Will you be at church Sunday?"

"Yes, if I'm not providentially hindered."

That has often been said. However, some object vigorously, saying that providence, meaning God, would surely not hinder anyone from his or her Christian responsibilities. What might someone mean who says, "If I'm not providentially hindered, I will do what God has commanded me to do"?

Conditions That Hinder

Paul was sometimes "hindered" from doing what he had planned to do for different reasons. Speaking of plans that were finished (preaching in regions where others had not been) and still other plans that had yet to be completed (delivering a contribution to the saints in Jerusalem), he said, "This is the reason why I have so often been hindered from coming to you" (Romans 15:22).

On another occasion, Paul wanted badly to return to the persecuted church in Thessalonica, which he had to leave hurriedly under duress from the persecutors. He said, "We wanted to come to you – I, Paul, again and again – but Satan hindered us" (1 Thessalonians 2:18).

So when Paul was hindered from doing something he had planned to do, in one case, he was hindered by his personal choice to do other things, and in another, Satan hindered him. In instances involving us, it might be either of those reasons, or it might just be other circumstances that hinder us. "Time and chance happen to them all" (Ecclesiastes 9:11).

Or might it be providence? Consider James' words:

> Come now, you who say, "Today or tomorrow we will go into such and such a town and spend a year there and trade and make a profit" – yet you do not know what tomorrow will bring. What is your life? For you are a mist that appears for a little time and then vanishes. Instead you ought to say, "If the Lord wills, we will live and do this or that." As it is, you boast in your arrogance. All such boasting is evil. (James 4:13-16)

So if I plan to attend a gospel meeting tomorrow but die this afternoon, an implication of James' words in this text is "It was not God's will that I do that." Was I, then, not "providentially hindered"?

God Is in Control

If we heed the message of James, we will not arrogantly presume on planning the future without taking God into consideration. "If God wills" is a good thing to say, or at least to have in awareness, whenever we are announcing our plans for the future. The wise man in Proverbs reminded us similarly: "The heart of man plans his way, but the LORD establishes his steps" (Proverbs 16:9). "Many are the plans in the mind of a man, but it is the purpose of the LORD that will stand" (19:21). "Do not boast about tomorrow, for you do not know what a day may bring" (27:1).

When the Scottish poet Robert Burns realized, while plowing a field, that he had uprooted and destroyed a mouse's nest, scattering her little ones, he wrote "To a Mouse." This now famous poem contains the often-quoted truth "The best laid schemes o' mice an' men gang aft a-gley" or, in plain American English, "often don't work out." The devotional classic, *The Imitation of Christ*, usually ascribed to Thomas à Kempis (1380–1471), has the famous line "For man proposes, but God disposes."

The Latin phrase *Deo volente*, "God willing," or its abbreviation, D.V., was once used frequently, especially in writing, when someone's intentions for the future were stated. I find myself almost unable to say anything about the future without some kind of qualifying phrase such as "Lord willing" or, at least, "If all goes well." When Paul stopped by Ephesus briefly, intending to return on his next (third) journey, he did the same: "But on taking leave of them he said, 'I will return to you if God wills,' and he set sail from Ephesus" (Acts 18:21). James' point, however, is not so much to get us to say a particular thing as it is to remind us that we are not in control; God is.

The Principle of "Perhaps"

Providence does not just hinder. Sometimes God somehow orders circumstances to bring about blessings in our lives. It is safe and biblical to say God frequently does that. It is more problematic to look back on a particular circumstance and say, "God did that." Even the inspired apostle Paul would only say "perhaps" God did that.

Onesimus was a runaway slave from the city of Colossae who, like many others in his situation, went to Rome. There, he met Paul, who converted him to Christ, and Onesimus became a regular companion and valuable helper of Paul during Paul's house arrest (Acts 28:16, 30-31; Philemon 10-13). When Paul learned that Onesimus had run away from Philemon, a brother in Christ whom Paul had converted during his stay in Ephesus (Acts 19:10; Philemon 10), Paul wrote to Philemon that he was sending Onesimus back, no longer as a slave but "as a beloved brother" (v. 16). Paul told Philemon, "For this perhaps is why he was parted from you for a while, that you might have him back forever" (v. 15). It seemed God's hand was behind it all. Paul, at least, thought that likely. But the most he would say about it was "perhaps" (v. 15).

To escape the command to kill all male Hebrew babies, Moses' mother put him in a reed basket at the edge of the river. His sister, Miriam, was charged to stay nearby. Moses was found by Pharaoh's daughter, who accepted Miriam's offer to find a woman of the Hebrews to nurse him. So Moses was nourished by his mother and evidently taught by her about the Lord, and she was paid by Pharaoh's house to do it. Providence? Undoubtedly? At least, perhaps.

A series of circumstances, several seemingly coincidental, brought about my appointment as dean of the V.P. Black College of Biblical Studies at Faulkner University. When I mentally recount them in my mind, I see "perhaps" the providential hand of God.

Wherever you find yourself at work – whether as a barber, an engineer, a construction worker, a teacher, an accountant or a waitress – trace in your mind the circumstances that brought you to whatever opportunities your situation affords you for doing good for the Lord and His kingdom. See if "perhaps" you see the hand of God in those circumstances. "Look carefully then how you walk, not as unwise but as wise, making the best use of the time, because the days are evil" (Ephesians 5:15-16). As you do that, God's providential care will be with you, regardless of whether you recognize it in particular instances.

Questions

1. What kinds of things, besides providence, may hinder our plans?

2. What objection do some raise to the idea that anyone might be "providentially hindered" from being at a congregational assembly, for example?

3. What are some of the implications of James' admonition, "You ought to say, 'If the Lord wills, we will live and do this or that' "?

4. What does Proverbs say about human plans?

5. Why is recognizing God's providential activity in specific instances "perhaps"?

6. What did Paul think providence "perhaps" brought about in regard to Philemon and Onesimus?

7. How did providence perhaps work in the infancy of Moses and with what purpose?

For Discussion

1. What do you think people usually mean when they speak of being "providentially hindered"?

2. What special opportunities for doing good are available to you in your present situation? Do you attribute any of those opportunities to providence?

3. Does God being with us, helping us and protecting us depend on us being able to know when and how He does so?

3

PROVIDENCE
and Free Will

According to James 4:13-17, if I die today, that means it was not God's will, at least in some sense, for me to do what I had planned to do tomorrow. That, then, raises another question: Was it God's will that I die? For a proper response to that and similar questions, we need to explore some different ways God's will can be understood.

Three Categories of God's Will

Leslie D. Weatherhead, an English Methodist preacher, suggests, with good common sense and scriptural reasoning, that there are three separate categories of God's will. According to Weatherhead, God has an intentional will, a circumstantial will, and an ultimate will.[1]

1. God's Intentional Will

A word about God's intentional will was spoken by Jesus at the conclusion of Matthew's account of the parable of the lost sheep. The shepherd reclaims the lost and rejoices, and Jesus added, "So it is not the will of my Father who is in heaven that one of these little ones should perish" (Matthew 18:14). God's "intentional will" is what He specifically desires and will, therefore, work to accomplish.

It denotes a serious misunderstanding to talk as if God's intentional will is at work when babies die or a drunken driver kills a faithful Christian. A preacher once said, at the funeral of a 6-year-old girl named Rose who had tragically drowned, "Heaven needed added beauty, so God reached down to earth and plucked a lovely Rose for His garden in Paradise." The preacher meant well and thought he was being complimentary, but if I had been that father, I would not have found that comforting.

If that is how God orders the world, God would be easy to despise and reject. Job suffered many losses and cruelties, but unlike some people today, "In all this Job did not sin or charge God with wrong" (Job 1:22). The King James Version says, "Job sinned not, nor charged God foolishly." Let us be careful not to charge God foolishly by speaking of the will of God in ways that imply God intentionally wills calamity or hurtful evil.

Because our Sovereign God by His sovereign choice made man and woman with free will, God's intentional will can be and often is thwarted by our sin and rebellion. Murder, war, theft (whether with a gun or by manipulating figures), abortion, exploitation of other humans for greed: Call these acts evil; maybe even attribute them in some sense to Satan. But do not say they are God's will in such a way as to imply that God desired they should occur or made them happen.

2. God's Circumstantial Will

Of things evil people do and even of natural calamities, such as tornados and earthquakes, we may perhaps say, "They were within the will of God." Surely a sovereign, all-powerful God could prevent such things if He wished. Weatherhead suggests God has a "circumstantial will."

A father and son agree that the son should pursue a business career and inherit his father's successful business. That is the father's intentional will. But if a war intervenes and the father and son then agree that the son should join the armed forces and fight for their country's freedom, that becomes the father's circumstantial will.

One result of Adam and Eve's sin in the Garden of Eden was a curse on woman, on man and on the ground (Genesis 3). It was not God's intentional will that sin enter the world, but it was His circumstantial will that sinful humanity not live forever in a world infected with sin and its consequences. So disease, calamity and death entered the world as God's circumstantial will.

We do not think of illness as the will of God in the sense that we should refuse to fight against it. On the contrary, we marshal our resources and best minds to cure illnesses and postpone pain and death. So circumstances changed with the introduction of sin into the world, a change not in accord with God's intentional will but brought about by the rebellion of His freewill creatures. Since God does not will that mankind live forever in a sin-cursed world, the ills that produce disease and death are within God's circumstantial will.

3. God's Ultimate Will

Job, after a lengthy dialogue with his friends and with God, expressed the truth of God's ultimate will: "I know that you can do all things, and that no purpose of yours can be thwarted" (Job 42:2).

Judas betrayed Jesus into the hands of His enemies. Judas' motives and aim were evil, and his deed was dastardly, but he did not thwart God's will. Actually, he helped accomplish the ultimate will of God for Jesus to die for the sins of mankind. The same is true of all who were involved in the crucifixion of Christ. Peter proclaimed on Pentecost, "This Jesus, delivered up according to the definite plan and foreknowledge of God, you crucified and killed by the hands of lawless men" (Acts 2:23).

God's omnipotence does not mean that everything that happens is His will in the sense of His intention. It does mean that neither we nor all the powers of hell can ultimately defeat Him.

The Freedom to Choose

God created us, male and female, in His image (Genesis 1:27). It is logical to conclude that He gave us freedom to choose good or evil so that we may love and have fellowship with Him because we want to, not because we have to or otherwise have no choice. He did not impose His will on us. Although omnipotent, He chose to limit Himself in that way. We are not robots. Our lives are not predetermined by fate or karma – or even by God.

Calvinism, which emphasizes the doctrine of predestination, grows out of a strong conviction that, because God is sovereign, if He wills anything, it has to be. From that, it is supposed by some that every detail of our lives, including but not limited to our salvation or condemnation, is predetermined by God. There is much disagreement among Calvinists, however, as to how that all works out in life, as illustrated perhaps by the person who quoted his grandmother, saying, "What is to be will be, whether it happens or not."

Does God have a plan for your life? Yes.

He plans for you to be saved from sin. "God our Savior ... desires all people to be saved and to come to the knowledge of the truth" (1 Timothy 2:3-4). "The Lord is ... patient toward you, not wishing that any should perish, but that all should reach repentance" (2 Peter 3:9). He plans for you to glorify Him. In a children's Bible class, the kids are asked, "Why were we made?" They are taught to answer, "To glorify God!" That is scriptural: "Or do you not know that your body is a temple of the Holy Spirit within you, whom you have from God? You are not your own, for you were bought with a price. So glorify God in your body" (1 Corinthians 6:19-20). Finally, He plans for all the redeemed to be "holy and blameless before him" (Ephesians 1:4).

Many, however, believe God has planned every person's life from the major details – such as where to go to school, whom to marry, where to live and work – down to the minutest details – such as what to eat for dinner, which shirt to buy, and so on. It is further urged that to be happy and find fulfillment, all people must find out what God has planned for them – only so can they be "in the center of God's will" and only so can they be truly blessed and successful.

It is common to hear from devoutly religious friends such expressions as "God led me here, and I am exactly where He wants me to be"; "Please pray that I will find the summer job God wants me to have"; and "Lord, help us find and recognize the man you have prepared and called to be our preacher." What is striking is how absent similar language is from Scripture.

Certainly there was supernatural guidance of the apostles on particular occasions such as when Paul and Silas were led to Troas to receive the Macedonian call in a vision. But even for the apostles, that was not the norm. On Paul's second missionary journey, he, Silas and Timothy established churches in both Thessalonica and Berea. But Paul was soon run out of both places by persecutors. Leaving his companions behind, Paul went on to Athens, but he wrote back to Thessalonica to say, "Therefore when we could bear it no longer, we were willing to be left behind at Athens alone, and we sent Timothy, our brother and God's co-worker in the gospel of Christ, to establish and exhort you in your faith" (1 Thessalonians 3:1-2).

"We were willing." "We thought it best" (NASB). "We decided" (ERV). How was their decision made? They thought it best. They had good reasons for that thought. They were concerned about their converts' endurance under persecution. They decided sending Timothy was the best means for meeting their concerns.

As Paul awaited trial before Nero in Rome, he was refreshed by the company of Epaphroditus, who had brought good tidings and gifts from Philippi. But Epaphroditus became ill and nearly died. Paul decided to send him home and explained it like this:

> I have thought it necessary to send to you Epaphroditus my brother and fellow worker and fellow soldier, and your messenger and minister to my need, for he has been longing for you all and has been distressed because you heard that he was ill. (Philippians 2:25-26)

Paul did not say he "felt led" to send Epaphroditus home or that God had told him to do so. He said, "I have thought it necessary." Again, he had good reasons to think so: Epaphroditus was eager to get home (Philippians 2:26); Paul wanted to turn the Philippians' anxiety for their messenger into joy (v. 28); and Paul needed him as a messenger to take his "thank-you letter" to the Philippians. In Paul's wisdom (common sense), he determined that sending Epaphroditus was the best way to accomplish important spiritual goals.

More Than One Right Choice

God certainly has a moral will, and He has clearly expressed that will in Scripture. However, when we are faced with choices not involving morality, God has given us the freedom to choose between more than one right option and urges us to use our wisdom. There are many good places to live and serve God and many occupations that offer opportunities of doing good. The idea that God has chosen a specific place for every individual to serve and that every person must discover this place in order to be living and working "in the center of God's will" is not taught in the Bible.

In the earliest days of my full-time preaching, a good friend and mentor urged my wife, Winnie, and me to go with him to Japan as missionaries. We came close to committing and going. Those were still the immediate post-World War II years, and Japan was a fertile field. Did we go against God's will by not going to Japan at that time? Was the work we did in Mississippi God's will for us in those days? Would it have been wrong for us to go to Japan instead? None of the above.

Consider the many choices of Adam and Eve in the Garden of Eden. "And the LORD God commanded the man, saying, 'You may surely eat of every tree of the garden, but of the tree of the knowledge of good and evil you shall not eat, for in the day that you eat of it you shall surely die' " (Genesis 2:16-17). Adam and Eve's moral choice was clear. They were not to eat of the tree of the knowledge of good and evil. But otherwise, they had complete freedom of choice.

Suppose Adam had pressed God and said, "I know I am not to eat of the tree of the knowledge of good and evil, but in order to be in your perfect will, which of the other trees would you have me to eat of first?" Would God have not reiterated, "You may surely eat of every tree of the garden"? There is no reason to suppose that eating any one fruit would have pleased God more than another. The choice was left to Adam's personal taste and preference.

Even in regard to marriage, while there are certainly moral choices to be made and immoral choices to be avoided, within the range of Christians eligible to be married, Paul made it clear that we are free to decide even whether to marry as well as whom to marry. Under certain conditions, one choice is "good"; under different conditions, the other "is better" (1 Corinthians 7:8-9). A widow who follows the moral directions of Scripture "is free to be married to whom she wishes" (v. 39).

Making Wise Choices

God promises Christians wisdom for the asking. "If any of you lacks wisdom, let him ask God, who gives generously to all without reproach, and it will be given him" (James 1:5). However, wisdom is not the same as specific information. James did not promise that God will whisper in our ears or give us an unmistakable emotional nudge to tell us which job offer to take or which of diverging paths to follow.

The kind of wisdom God gives is delineated later in the same epistle: "But the wisdom from above is first pure, then peaceable, gentle, open to reason, full of mercy and good fruits, impartial and sincere" (James 3:17). Wisdom may be defined as the ability to make good use of the knowledge we possess. "Common sense" is another good name for it, although even in calling it that we might acknowledge it is none too common. One of my uncles called it "horse sense" and then would explain, "Horse sense is the good sense horses have that keeps them from betting on people."

Paul, writing by inspiration, specifically declared that Christians, of all people, ought to be competent to make wise decisions. He rebuked the Corinthians for going to law against one another before unbelieving judges and said: "Or do you not know that the saints will judge the world? And if the world is to be judged by you, are you incompetent to try trivial cases?" (1 Corinthians 6:2).

In decisions that do not involve morality, we have God-given freedom. We should use spiritual discernment and act, as Paul did. If we do so genuinely desiring to seek God and His righteousness above all else, then we can enter into whatever decision we make confident that it will be pleasing to God; His blessing will be with us in whatever choices we make.

Paul was on the way to deliver the contribution he had taken up among the Gentile churches for the famine-struck Christians in Jerusalem when the Holy Spirit warned, through prophets speaking to Paul, that chains and maybe death awaited him there. His brothers and sisters in the Lord wept, urging him not to go. Paul answered: "What are you doing, weeping and breaking my heart? For I am ready not only to be imprisoned but even to die in Jerusalem for the name of the Lord Jesus" (Acts 21:13).

Then Luke, who was accompanying Paul, recorded, "And since he would not be persuaded, we ceased and said, 'Let the will of the Lord be done'" (Acts 21:13-14). In that case, though they could not have known it at the time, "the will of the Lord" turned out to be for Paul to go to Rome as a prisoner instead of as a freely traveling evangelist. But as Paul testified in Philippians, perhaps more good was done in critical places than could have been done otherwise (cf. Philippians 1:13).

A popular keynote speaker at a well-attended workshop spoke on the importance of obeying God. I thought to myself, "Great topic." But he began describing the process by which he came to work at the large church where he was currently the preacher. They were constantly after him to come there, and he "felt" God was pushing him in that direction. However, he was comfortable where he was and did not want to move. Only when he finally "yielded to God" and went did he find happiness and peace. "Obey God," he said, "and find happiness."

When Jesus said "If you love me, you will keep my commandments" (John 14:15), He was not talking about obeying inclinations or strong inner impulses. He was not talking about the direction you think He might be "leading you" to work or serve. We obey Jesus by loving God with all of our being and our neighbor as ourselves, by feeding the hungry, by visiting the sick and lonely, and by heeding His commandments found in Scripture. God's Word is not conjured up out of our subjective consciousness.

The idea that God has planned a specific course of action for every individual concerning one's education, marriage, career, etc., is not biblical. We are to obey God in all things. We are to seek His kingdom and righteousness first (Matthew 6:33). We are to consider the interests of others as well as our own (Philippians 2:4). With those priorities considered, when we choose where to work or whom to marry or which road to take, we can choose what we believe is best. God will be with us and bless us.

A familiar story is told of a preacher who received a call to a bigger church with better financial support. One of the church members went to the minister's house and asked his daughter whether her family would be leaving. She replied: "I think so. Daddy is upstairs praying, but Mama is downstairs packing." What that story primarily illustrates is that mundane factors like salary, benefits and prestige affect our decisions, whatever else we may be relying on to help us decide.

Preachers are under the same obligation to support their families as every other Christian (1 Timothy 5:8). When that minimum obligation is met, however, dedicated servants of the Lord make decisions on where to work considering other primary factors, including need and quality of opportunity. In biographical sketches of pioneer restoration preachers, several turned down opportunities for more support and larger audiences on grounds similar to this: "You will be able to attract many to that work with those benefits. The Christians here would have a much more difficult time finding someone else to work with them."

In summary, in those areas where there is no divine command or moral principle involved, the Christian is free and responsible for his or her personal choices. Any decision made within the moral will of God is acceptable to God. Our Sovereign God sovereignly chose to create us with moral sensibilities; we are free to choose either good or evil. Then when we love and obey Him, it will be because we want to rather than because we have to or are pre-programmed to do so. It does not seem strange to me that a Sovereign God desires to have eternal fellowship with such sons and daughters.

Questions

1. Would it ever be God's intentional will for a drunk driver to kill a faithful Christian or anyone?

2. How did Adam and Eve's sin, and the curses that followed, change the will of God?

3. What is the difference between "It was the will of God" and "It was within the will of God"?

4. What is God's will for our lives? For what purpose did He make us?

5. Has God planned for each of us what our careers should be, where we should work, and whom we should marry? Can we be happy only if we find His will in each instance and follow it?

6. On what basis did Paul decide to send Timothy back to Thessalonica?

7. On what basis did Paul decide to send the ailing Epaphroditus to Philippi?

8. Is it necessary to always follow God's stated moral will?

9. How can we get wisdom?

10. What kind of wisdom, according to James, does God provide?

For Discussion

1. Name and define or illustrate each of the three categories of God's will as described in this chapter.

2. Is God any less sovereign because He has allowed humans to have free will? Explain your answer.

3. If humans have free will, do they have the power to thwart the ultimate will of God? Explain your answer.

4. Jesus said, "If you love me, you will keep my commandments" (John 14:15). What commandments was He talking about?

4

THE PROMISE
of Good

God has granted us "through the knowledge of him who called us to his own glory and excellence ... precious and very great promises" (2 Peter 1:3-4). Some of these promises, as recorded in Scripture, clearly imply God's providence – His continued activity in the world on behalf of His faithful children. One such promise is Romans 8:28: "And we know that for those who love God all things work together for good, for those who are called according to his purpose."

It is a given that bad things happen to good people. The patriarch Job is a prime and powerful example of this. But no matter what happens to the faithful children of God, God's providential care continues.

"We Know"

"And **we know** that for those who love God all
things work together for good, for those who are called
according to his purpose" (Romans 8:28).

"We know" that for those who love God all things work together for good. How do we know? J.W. McGarvey suggests, "Partly by experience but primarily by revelation." [1]

Many of us have had experiences that validate this promise. When I was 10 years old, I contracted rheumatic fever. The danger of that disease to the heart was well-known, but modern antibiotics with which to treat it were not. My wise and knowledgeable doctor prescribed sulfur drugs and bed rest, and I recovered with no heart damage. But the whole year I would have been in the fifth grade, I was at home, confined to bed.

My friends in the neighborhood gathered in the yards and street outside my bedroom window most afternoons and evenings until dark, playing kick the can and stick ball. At 10 and 11 years old, I was not theologically astute. More unexpressed than articulated, I fretted over having to lie in bed while my friends were outside playing the games I wanted to be playing. It did not occur to me to wonder, "What good can possibly come from this?" I certainly saw no good in it at the time.

When I picked back up in the fifth grade a year later, I was with a new teacher and new friends and classmates. I encountered vastly different experiences than I would have if I had not lost that year out of my life. Undoubtedly, that changed the course of my life. There is no way I can know what my life would be – where I would be living, what I would be doing, whether I would be married or to whom – except that it would certainly be entirely different from what it is now. And I love my life as it is. I love the path that has brought me to where I am in life. I love my work, my wife, my children and grandchildren. Truly, my year of sickness has worked for my good.

Romans 8:28 does not say that God made me have rheumatic fever so that my life would turn out as it has. Bad things happen for a variety of reasons. Sometimes specific sins bring calamitous consequences: Sexual immorality often results in sexually transmitted diseases and even death. Other calamities happen to innocent people because of the sins of others: A drunken driver kills and maims a godly family. Still other disasters happen seemingly at random. The Preacher said, "Time and chance happen to them all" (Ecclesiastes 9:11).

Sin is the ultimate cause even of the tragedies that happen at random. When Adam sinned, death spread to all mankind, and with it came all the germs and viruses that cause disease and death and the laws of cause and effect that wreak havoc on human bodies when automobile or other accidents occur. "Death spread to all men, because all sinned" (Romans 5:12). Regardless of why disastrous events occur, however, God can and will – because He has promised to – bring good from them to those who love Him.

"For Those Who Love God"

"And we know that **for those who love God** all things work together for good, for those who are called according to his purpose" (Romans 8:28).

We know that "for those who love God" and "for those who are called according to his purpose" all things work together for good (Romans 8:28). Those phrases describe the same people. Who are those who love God? "Whoever has my commandments and keeps them, he it is who loves me" (John 14:21). That does not mean "those who are sinless," for no one is. But it does mean "those who follow a lifestyle consistent with the way Scripture teaches us to live."

Christians in Rome were addressed as those "loved by God and called to be saints" (Romans 1:7). God has "saved us and called us to a holy calling, not because of our works but because of his own purpose and grace, which he gave us in Christ Jesus before the ages began" (2 Timothy 1:9). Romans 8:28 is not a promise, therefore, that everything always works out great for everybody. It is a specific promise of something God does for His faithful children.

"All Things"

"And we know that for those who love God **all things** work together for good, for those who are called according to his purpose" (Romans 8:28).

We know that for those who love God "all things" work together for good. These words immediately precede a panoramic description of redemption from God's perspective:

> And we know that for those who love God all things work together for good, for those who are called according to his

purpose. For those whom he foreknew he also predestined to be conformed to the image of his Son, in order that he might be the firstborn among many brothers. And those whom he predestined he also called, and those whom he called he also justified, and those whom he justified he also glorified. (Romans 8:28-30)

Some maintain that the "all things" that work together for good are the elements in that passage that result in our glorification. They say, then, to apply this passage to sickness, death, financial losses and such like is to take it out of context.

However, a general statement of truth can apply to specific elements in a context and still have broader application to other things as well. Second John 9 – "Everyone who goes on ahead and does not abide in the teaching of Christ, does not have God" – specifically applies to some who were denying the humanity of Christ, "the coming of Jesus Christ in the flesh" (v. 7). But the New Testament as a whole makes it clear that there are other serious errors to which the same warning applies. Claiming circumcision as necessary for salvation nullifies the sufficiency of the cross (Galatians 5:11). Forbidding marriage and commanding abstinence from certain foods is the teaching of demons (1 Timothy 4:1-3). Teaching that the resurrection had already happened upset the faith of some (2 Timothy 2:17-18).

"Tribulation, or distress, or persecution, or famine, or nakedness, or danger, or sword" are all referred to in the larger context of Romans 8 (v. 35). Nothing that can happen to a faithful child of God is beyond the power of God to cause to produce a blessing.

"Work Together"

"And we know that for those who love God all
things **work together** for good, for those who are called
according to his purpose" (Romans 8:28).

We know that for those who love God all things "work together" for good. It may take a comprehensive view of many events over several years to see clearly how things have worked together for good. Loving chocolate candy and chocolate cake, I once tasted some cocoa. Ugh. It was unbelievably bitter. Butter is not good alone. Even sugar cloys if you get too much of it. But when all the ingredients are properly combined by a master chef, they can make a delicious dessert.

Patiently waiting for the Lord to keep His promise, which He will do in His own good time, enables us to see the good that eventually comes from even the worst calamities. "They who wait for the LORD shall renew their strength; they shall mount up with wings like eagles; they shall run and not be weary; they shall walk and not faint" (Isaiah 40:31). Patience is a virtue. We need to learn to wait and see what the Lord has in store for us.

"For Good"

"And we know that for those who love God all
things work together **for good**, for those who are called
according to his purpose" (Romans 8:28).

We know that for those who love God all things work together "for good." What we might define as good and what God might define as good may not always be the same. We might be thinking of what is good in the short run, whereas God might be working toward our eternal good. "For I consider that the sufferings of this present time are not worth comparing with the glory that is to be revealed to us" (Romans 8:18). In any case, Romans 8:28 is a promise made by a God "who never lies" (Titus 1:2). He will fulfill it.

When Onesimus ran away from the enforced servitude of Philemon to Rome, where he met Paul and was converted, Paul believed that it may "perhaps" have been God's way of bringing Onesimus back to Philemon – no longer as a slave but as a beloved brother (Philemon 15-16). Just so, when calamity somehow turns out to bring unexpected blessings, we can "perhaps" attribute it to the providence of God. But whatever may be true in an individual instance, "we know that for those who love God all things work together for good" (Romans 8:28).

Questions

1. Does Romans 8:28 say God makes bad things happen in our lives so He can bring good from them? If not, what does it say instead?

2. What are some of the reasons bad things happen to good people?

3. When should we take responsibility for the calamities in our lives?

4. Does the promise of Romans 8:28 apply to all people? If not, then to whom does it apply?

5. What are included in the "all things" that God works to the Christian's good?

6. In some cases, we might only see how God has brought blessings from bad things after several decades. Might it be, in other cases, that only in eternity it can be seen?

For Discussion

1. Is it correct to say that the promise of Romans 8:28 requires God to be active in our world and in our personal circumstances?

2. Are there instances in your life that, as you look back, cause you to think that Romans 8:28 has been fulfilled in your life?

3. God works all things together for good. How might His idea of what is good differ from ours?

5

THE PROMISE
of Prayer

n Psalm 119:160, the psalmist addressed God and said, "The sum
of your word is truth." More than one correct application could
be made from that observation, but the statement surely includes
the meaning that we must see all that the Bible says about a subject
before we are equipped to understand fully that subject

The subject of salvation is a case in point. Is saving sinners something
God does entirely on His own initiative, imposing no necessary conditions for sinners to meet? Or is salvation just orientated around good
works – the good go to heaven, and evildoers go to hell?

Many scriptures emphasize Christ's atoning sacrifice and God's grace
as the basis of salvation (e.g., Ephesians 2:8-9; Romans 6:23; 11:5-6).
These are cited by some as if to imply salvation is all God's doing and
we have no part in it at all. However, many other scriptures emphasize
that we must obey God, care for the poor, and live pure lives to be
saved (e.g., Matthew 7:21; 25:34-36; Acts 2:40; Philippians 2:12). These
are sometimes cited as if to suggest we must be saved by our personal
effort and precise obedience.

God's Word does not contradict itself. Scripture must be understood
in context and measured by other scriptural truths. Disputants do the

Bible a disservice when they line up scripture against scripture in a kind of "choose which scriptures you prefer" battle, as though one set opposed the other. It takes the sum of God's Word on the subject of salvation to know God's truth concerning it.

What Scripture Says About Prayer

The same principle applies to discovering and understanding God's truth about answering His children's prayers. A considerable array of verses can be cited that can be understood as meaning every prayer prayed properly by a faithful child of God will be answered affirmatively. For instance,

> • "Ask, and it will be given to you; seek, and you will find; knock, and it will be opened to you. For everyone who asks receives, and the one who seeks finds, and to the one who knocks it will be opened. Or which one of you, if his son asks him for bread, will give him a stone? Or if he asks for a fish, will give him a serpent? If you then, who are evil, know how to give good gifts to your children, how much more will your Father who is in heaven give good things to those who ask him!" (Matthew 7:7-11).

> • "And whatever you ask in prayer, you will receive, if you have faith" (Matthew 21:22).

> • "The prayer of a righteous person has great power as it is working" (James 5:16).

Many Christians may quickly say: "I have found those promises to be true. I have enjoyed and am thankful for many answered prayers." Other faithful Christians, however, remember times when they prayed fervently for a loved one to get well, and that person died anyway. Others have suffered setbacks – some family related, some financial – about which they believe they prayed to no avail. Are we to conclude that those whose prayers were not answered did not have enough faith or that they prayed with the wrong motive? The truth is that the promises we read about answered prayers are true, but they are not the whole truth. They are not the sum of the Bible's teaching about prayer.

God Knows What We Need

Paul was faithful and pleaded with the Lord three times to remove an infirmity that he believed hindered his work; a "thorn in the flesh," he called it. But God did not remove it (2 Corinthians 12:7-8). As an apostle of Christ, Paul had the advantage of special revelations from God and His Spirit that are not given to us. He told us in 2 Corinthians about his repeated prayers for the removal of his "thorn" and about the blessings his prayers brought even though the infirmity was not removed.

Although we do not have the advantage of the same kind of direct revelation God gave Paul, we can learn something about how God works from Paul's situation. Specifically, Paul explained that God's purpose in not removing his "thorn" was to keep him from being too proud or puffed up by the many special revelations he had received (2 Corinthians 12:7-10).

Sometimes what we ask for is not really what we need. Jesus said, "Which one of you, if his son asks him for bread, will give him a stone?" (Matthew 7:9). In Jesus' day, bread was often made from little round balls of dough, which were cooked in a hole in the ground in which a fire was laid and to which stones were added. The stones were made hot by the fire, and the heat from the stones would then cook the bread. As the delicious hot bread was being taken up for eating, a child might see one of the hot stones and, mistaking it for bread, point to it eagerly: "I want that big one, Daddy." The father – older and wiser, knowing what the child was asking for was not really what he wanted – would withhold the stone and supply the real need.

After three fervent requests to have his infirmity removed, Paul said that God answered him with these words: "My grace is sufficient for you" (2 Corinthians 12:9). There has been much speculation about what Paul's thorn in the flesh may have been. Many think they can build a strong case for a particular answer, but no one knows for sure. Similarly, we do not know what the grace was that God gave Paul instead of removing the thorn. This could have been the grace that brings salvation; Paul often rejoiced in that grace. Paul also considered his ministry – his apostleship to the Gentiles – a gift of grace. Or this grace could have been some other favor specifically granted in lieu of removing the thorn.

Whatever it was, God said it was enough, sufficient. Paul, in effect, said he would rather continue to have the thorn than forgo the favor God had given him. From this episode in Paul's life, we learn that God sometimes does not do exactly as we have asked because He knows things we do not know; what we ask may be more harmful than beneficial.

God's promise to hear and respond to His children's prayers further implies His present activity in the world on our behalf – in other words, His providence.

God's Answer Is Always Better

When God withholds what we have asked for, He may give something else that, on later reflection, we realize is better.

Jesus Christ was faithful and prayed fervently, three times, for something He did not receive (Matthew 26:36-46). He pleaded for the cup of suffering and condemnation He knew He was about to endure to be removed. That night in the garden – the night of His betrayal, culminating in the mockery of a trial and His crucifixion – was a dark night not only for Jesus but also for His apostles.

After Jesus' death, His followers thought all the hopes and dreams they had placed in Jesus had failed and were undone. "We had hoped that he was the one to redeem Israel," two of His disciples said (Luke 24:21). Yet when it was all over, what everyone thought was a dark night of despair and unanswered prayer showed itself to be, instead, a time of victory and redemption, validated by Jesus' resurrection from the dead.

Significantly, Jesus' prayers to the Father in the garden were not only "Remove this cup from me"; He added each time, "Nevertheless, not my will, but yours, be done" (Luke 22:42). "Your will be done" may be said by some people as a kind of escape clause when prayers are offered for the seriously or terminally ill. The thought may be "They are not going to get well, so we better add 'according to Your will.'" Rather than an afterthought, however, the prayer for God's will to be done ought to be the first and foremost plea in all of our prayers.

Jesus taught us to so pray, "Your will be done, on earth as it is in heaven" (Matthew 6:10). To pray for God's will to be done is to pray for the best possible outcome. As in Jesus' case, it may not seem good for the moment, but its culmination is victory.

Thursday night was despair in the garden. Friday night was death and burial. But Sunday came with resurrection and triumph. In the dark times, what seems to be defeat and despair, we should be faithful, keep on loving God, and keep praying.

Questions

1. What does the Bible say will happen when, as faithful children of the Father, we ask, knock and seek?

2. Does the Bible teach that every prayer asked by faithful children of the Father will be answered affirmatively?

3. Why did God not remove the infirmity Paul prayed three times to have removed?

4. What did God do instead of removing Paul's "thorn"?

5. In the Garden of Gethsemane, what did Jesus pray three times not to have to bear?

6. What did Jesus add to His prayer all three times?

7. How does Jesus' resurrection story give us hope in times of despair and seemingly unanswered prayer?

For Discussion

1. A few Christians have maintained that prayer cannot change God's mind or cause anything to happen that would not have happened anyway. So when asked why we should pray, they reply: "Because we are commanded to. The only thing prayer can change is the person praying." How would you respond to such an idea?

2. What has been your experience in prayer? Have you always received just what you asked for, or have you sometimes prayed fervently for things that never occurred? Which experience do you read about in the Bible?

3. Why was it God's will for Christ to go to the cross? Was it also Christ's will?

6

Other Biblical
PROMISES

In addition to the promises about answering prayer and about working all things to the faithful Christian's good, three other promises imply God's active participation in the affairs of this world: (1) We will never be tempted beyond our ability to bear it (1 Corinthians 10:13). (2) Food, shelter and clothing will be provided to those who seek first the kingdom of God and His righteousness (Matthew 6:33). (3) God will never forsake us, but will care for us and protect us (Hebrews 13:5-6).

Help in Temptation

"No temptation has overtaken you that is not common to man. God is faithful, and he will not let you be tempted beyond your ability, but with the temptation he will also provide the way of escape, that you may be able to endure it" (1 Corinthians 10:13).

What circumstances must God manipulate and how many people and things must He use to see that we are never tempted beyond our ability to endure – and that every temptation is accompanied by a way of escape? Who can know? Who could say? But who would deny that the promise is kept?

Along with the unknowns are some certainties. Satan is the one who tempts, in the sense of enticing us to do evil (1 Thessalonians 3:5); God never does that (James 1:13). Satan will sometimes use agents – even friends and co-workers, who become his agents unwittingly (Peter, for example, in Matthew 16:22-23) – to cause such enticements. However, where Satan does have persuasive powers, he does not have coercive powers. "The devil made me do it" is never true. Satan cannot make anyone do anything. God, on the other hand, has coercive power but has chosen not use it. He made us freewill creatures, and He will not violate that by making us do things against our will.

By whatever means He accomplishes what He does – strengthening us, working in and through us – He does not violate our free will. But He, too, uses persuasive powers – people and circumstances, including open and closed doors – to entice us toward doing what is good. God "desires all people to be saved and to come to the knowledge of the truth" (1 Timothy 2:4). Now that we are reconciled through Jesus and are His children, He will freely give us all things needed (Romans 5:10-11). His promise is sure, but as with most promises of God, He expects us to cooperate. When we are tempted, instead of looking for a way to yield without getting caught, we need to look for the way of escape that God has promised He will provide. Consider the following ways to cooperate with God in order to handle temptation.

Flee

One way to handle temptation is to flee, as Joseph did from Potiphar's wife. The Bible says, "flee from idolatry" (1 Corinthians 10:14); "flee youthful passions" (2 Timothy 2:22); "flee from fornication" (1 Corinthians 10:14); and – after mentioning the desire to be rich, the love of money, and greediness – "O man of God, flee these things" (1 Timothy 6:11).

The best bus drivers to hire for a mountainous route are not the ones who can drive closest to the edge without going over; rather, they are the ones who stay as far from the edge as possible. Do not go to a bar for fun and companionship. Avoid the flirtatious co-worker. Find something better to read or watch than the pornographic magazine or movie. Take your spouse or a trusted Christian friend when you must go to events or places that may present temptations. Flee! Flee! Flee!

Study God's Word

The psalmist said, speaking to God, "I have stored up your word in my heart, that I might not sin against you" (Psalm 119:11). Jesus demonstrated the practicality and power of knowing and using the Word to resist temptation in His confrontation with the devil in the wilderness. For each temptation the devil presented, Jesus quoted the exact scripture that answered the temptation. As a result, "the devil left him" (Matthew 4:11). "Resist the devil, and he will flee from you" (James 4:7). There is no stronger weapon with which to resist temptation than the Word of God.

In order to store up the Word and have it available for such use, it is necessary to read it, study it diligently, meditate on it, and commit it to memory. The blessed man is the one whose "delight is in the law of the LORD, and on his law he meditates day and night" (Psalm 1:2). While a popular proverb says "You are what you eat," it is much more pertinent to observe "You are what you read." The constant reading of trash will result in a trashy mind that, in turn, will lead to a trashy life. Read and think on things that are true and good and holy, and your life will be lifted up. The Word of God is "able to build you up" (Acts 20:32).

Pray

When Jesus left His disciples in the garden while He went apart to agonize, He told them, "Pray that you may not enter into temptation" (Luke 22:40, 46). When the disciples asked Jesus to teach them to pray, He included in His model, "And lead us not into temptation" (11:2-4). Prayer is a powerful weapon against the devil and his wiles. The admonition "Resist the devil, and he will flee from you" is coupled with one to "draw near to God, and he will draw near to you" (James 4:7-8). Prayer is an effective way to draw close to God and call on His power and resources.

Pray regularly for strength to overcome temptation. When faced with a specific temptation, ask to be delivered from it. Pray for the ability to see and to take the "way of escape" God has promised to provide (1 Corinthians 10:13).

Keep Watch

Although Luke recorded Jesus' admonition to His disciples to pray to avoid temptation, both Matthew and Mark noted that Jesus added another admonition: "Watch and pray that you may not enter into temptation" (Matthew 26:41; Mark 14:38). The devil is a liar in the very essence of his being, and he is so proficient at lying that he is called "a liar and the father of lies" (John 8:44). He deceived Eve by his craftiness (2 Corinthians 11:3). He can even twist Scripture for his own purposes (Matthew 4:6). We are urged to be well-armored to defeat his schemes (Ephesians 6:11).

"The devil doesn't come to you ugly," one of my students used to say. He will look attractive. He will promise pleasure. He may be disguised as "an angel of light," and his servants may appear to be "servants of righteousness" (2 Corinthians 11:14-15). But all of Satan's apples have worms. The pleasure he promises is only temporary, and the life he promises is death – the lake of fire and brimstone. Do not be deceived. Sin is addictive. It has an enslaving power. "Hell and destruction are never full; so the eyes of man are never satisfied" (Proverbs 27:20 KJV). Sins adds to sin because sin never cries, "Enough!" Be alert. Be aware. Keep watch.

Fill Your Life With Good Things

Perhaps most important, when you are resisting something negative, consciously replace it with something positive. Do you remember the Lord's story about the unclean spirit who leaves a man but finds no resting place? Returning, it finds its former place swept and in order, but empty. "Then it goes and brings with it seven other spirits more evil than itself, and they enter and dwell there, and the last state of that person is worse than the first. So also will it be with this evil generation" (Matthew 12:45).

This story illustrates the point that getting rid of an evil or chasing away an enticement to evil is not enough. Something good must be put in its place. It is best not to dwell too long on temptations, even for the purpose of praying about them. Ask God for strength and deliverance, and then chase the temptations away from your mind by thinking about something positive or doing something good.

Quote a scripture. Think of a good deed, and go do it. Replace temptation toward an extramarital affair with loving attention to your spouse. Replace pornography with prayer and cursing with compliments. Sing a hymn. "Whatever is true, whatever is honorable, whatever is just, whatever is pure, whatever is lovely, whatever is commendable, if there is any excellence, if there is anything worthy of praise, think about these things" (Philippians 4:8).

Temptation is a universal fact of life. Being tempted does not mean you are evil; it simply means you are human. But no temptation brings the fruit of sin until it is welcomed and activated by sinful passions within ourselves. Therefore, watch, resist temptation with the Word, pray and replace temptation with godly thoughts and actions. By God's grace and mercy, there will always be a way of escape.

Provision of Life's Necessities

"But seek first the kingdom of God
and his righteousness, and all these things
will be added to you" (Matthew 6:33).

"All these things" includes food, drink and clothing (Matthew 6:31) – the basic necessities of life. Pagans seek after them, meaning their minds are set on those things; the things of the flesh are their priorities. But our heavenly Father knows we need those things (v. 32) and cares when we do not have them. However, He wants the things of the Spirit to be our priorities (cf. Romans 8:5-6). Jesus' message in Matthew 6 instructs His disciples not to fret or worry over food, shelter or clothing. Put God's righteousness and kingdom first, and as He feeds the birds of the heavens and clothes the flowers of the field, He will take care of our basic needs.

Obviously Jesus was not saying we have no need to work and save to provide for our physical needs. But He did mean that we should make God's will our foremost priority even if doing so appears to interfere with making a livelihood. Many are able to testify to incidents in their lives when they obeyed God first despite the fact that it looked like it would be bad for business – only to find the loss more than made up for by an unexpected windfall.

Other truths, however, need to be factored in to see the fullness of biblical truth regarding this promise. In a psalm that, throughout, promises temporal blessings to those who trust God, David said, "I have been young, and now am old, yet I have not seen the righteous forsaken or his children begging for bread" (Psalm 37:25). A Bible teacher in a Christian university read that verse; declared that he, like David, had never seen such a thing either; and expressed that he did not think anyone ever would. A student raised his hand and said, "But what about Lazarus, who lay hungry at the rich man's door?"

Every scripture, correctly understood in its context, is true, but sometimes another passage can throw additional light on a scripture or suggest looking at it from a different angle. Beginning with Job and continuing throughout Scripture, promises of temporal blessings lie side by side with warnings that Christians do not necessarily escape difficulty, calamity and hardship.

An atheist farmer, whose land lay next to a Christian's farm, tried an experiment one year. He set aside a plot of land and worked it only on Sundays while his Christian neighbor was at church. As harvest time came, he invited his neighbor to see his special field.

"You see the crop in this field?" he asked. "It is abundant! All the work on this field was done while you were wasting your time at church. What do you think now?"

The Christian just smiled and said, "I think God does not settle all of His accounts in October."

In answer to Peter's statement that he and the other apostles had left all to follow Him, Jesus said,

> Truly, I say to you, there is no one who has left house or brothers or sisters or mother or father or children or lands, for my sake and for the gospel, who will not receive a hundredfold now in this time, houses and brothers and sisters and mothers and children and lands, with persecutions, and in the age to come eternal life. (Mark 10:29-30)

That is a very real promise, and laying aside any claim that I have left all, I have seen it fulfilled many times over in my lifetime.

Having preached in congregations all over the U.S., I have dozens of "mothers" in many places who love me and hundreds of brothers and sisters who care for me and who would help me immediately in any difficulty. There is also a reminder in Jesus' promise, however, that some of God's blessings are beyond this world, and Christians will face tribulation and persecution. The Bible very plainly says, "Indeed, all who desire to live a godly life in Christ Jesus will be persecuted" (2 Timothy 3:12).

One of the main lessons of the rich man and Lazarus story, as told by Jesus, is found in the words of Abraham to the formerly rich man: "Child, remember that you in your lifetime received your good things, and Lazarus in like manner bad things; but now he is comforted here, and you are in anguish" (Luke 16:25). Heaven will erase life's inequities, but poverty, sickness and calamity do sometimes come to faithful Christians in this life.

Similar to the words of Psalm 34:12-16, Peter said:

> Whoever desires to love life and see good days, let him keep
> his tongue from evil and his lips from speaking deceit; let him
> turn away from evil and do good; let him seek peace and
> pursue it. For the eyes of the Lord are on the righteous, and
> his ears are open to their prayer. But the face of the Lord is
> against those who do evil. (1 Peter 3:10-12)

Christians are right to rely on God to providentially fulfill those promises, but they should temper them with "Indeed, all who desire to live a godly life in Christ Jesus will be persecuted" (2 Timothy 3:12).

Constant Care and Protection

> "Keep your life free from love of money, and be
> content with what you have, for he has said, 'I will
> never leave you nor forsake you.' So we can confidently
> say, 'The Lord is my helper; I will not fear; what can
> man do to me?' " (Hebrews 13:5-6).

In addition to being omnipotent and omniscient, God is omnipresent. Biblical mention of that attribute is sometimes meant to warn us that no evil deed or thought eludes His watchful eye, and there is no place to escape His righteous wrath. The prophet warned:

> I saw the Lord standing beside the altar, and he said: "Strike
> the capitals until the thresholds shake, and shatter them
> on the heads of all the people; and those who are left of
> them I will kill with the sword; not one of them shall flee
> away; not one of them shall escape. If they dig into Sheol,
> from there shall my hand take them; if they climb up to
> heaven, from there I will bring them down. If they hide
> themselves on the top of Carmel, from there I will search
> them out and take them; and if they hide from my sight at
> the bottom of the sea, there I will command the serpent,
> and it shall bite them. And if they go into captivity before
> their enemies, there I will command the sword, and it shall
> kill them; and I will fix my eyes upon them for evil and not
> for good." (Amos 9:1-4)

However, the mention of God's ability to be wherever we are and to
see everything we do wherever we are is most often meant as a comfort
and blessing to His faithful children. David used language reminiscent
of the warning of Amos, but for the opposite purpose:

> Where shall I go from your Spirit? Or where shall I flee
> from your presence? If I ascend to heaven, you are there! If
> I make my bed in Sheol, you are there! If I take the wings
> of the morning and dwell in the uttermost parts of the sea,
> even there your hand shall lead me, and your right hand
> shall hold me. If I say, "Surely the darkness shall cover me,
> and the light about me be night," even the darkness is not
> dark to you; the night is bright as the day, for darkness is
> as light with you. (Psalm 139:7-12)

God knows, remembers and rewards our smallest good deeds. "And
whoever gives one of these little ones even a cup of cold water because he is a disciple, truly, I say to you, he will by no means lose his
reward" (Matthew 10:42).

Jesus especially promised to be with us when we are carrying out
His will. He "came to seek and to save the lost" (Luke 19:10). He has
commissioned us to do the same: "Go therefore and make disciples
of all nations, baptizing them in the name of the Father and of the

Son and of the Holy Spirit, teaching them to observe all that I have commanded you" (Matthew 28:19-20). When we do this, He has promised to be with us "always, to the end of the age" (v. 20). If we know that we are doing what He has commanded us to do, we can know that He is with us in the doing of it.

A promise of presence and protection originally given to Joshua (Joshua 1:5) is certified by the writer of Hebrews to apply to all of God's faithful children: "Keep your life free from love of money, and be content with what you have, for he has said, 'I will never leave you nor forsake you.' So we can confidently say, 'The Lord is my helper; I will not fear; what can man do to me?' " (Hebrews 13:5-6). Putting the promise of God's continual presence in the context of contentment with our material comforts may be intended to remind us of Jesus' promise: "All these things shall be added to you" (Matthew 6:33). However, enabling us to say "I will not fear; what can man do to me?" speaks more to protection from harm.

In both Matthew 10:26-31 and Luke 12:4-7, Jesus told His disciples not to fear those who can kill the body. Interestingly, Luke added, "… and after that have nothing more that they can do" (v. 4). From a human standpoint, killing the body is the ultimate punishment. Only the Christian can dismiss death casually with "Is that all they can do?" That is because to the Christian the death of the body is not the real end. "I will warn you whom to fear," Jesus added, "fear him who, after he has killed, has authority to cast into hell" (v. 5). That undoubtedly means "Fear God."

Both Matthew and Luke told us that following this pronouncement, Jesus added His classic pronouncement of God's providential concern for His people: "Are not five sparrows sold for two pennies? And not one of them is forgotten before God. Why, even the hairs of your head are all numbered. Fear not; you are of more value than many sparrows" (Luke 12:6-7; cf. Matthew 10:29-31).

Every blessing of God's providence is dependent on our faith that no earthly calamity, including our death, can invalidate the righteousness of God by faith in Jesus Christ, which is our greatest and most valuable asset. Paul said all other things he had previously counted as assets were losses and rubbish by contrast (Philippians 3:4-10).

Faith that God providentially cares for all of His children is sustained by the realization that sometimes the promised blessing is realized only in eternity. "For I consider that the sufferings of this present time are not worth comparing with the glory that is to be revealed to us" (Romans 8:18).

Questions

1. What help are we promised in times of temptation?

2. How do we need to cooperate with God if we are to successfully resist temptation?

3. When we are tempted to do evil, who is doing the enticing?

4. What is wrong with the excuse "The devil made me do it"?

5. Give some examples of how we might seek God's kingdom and righteousness first, trusting Him to supply our material needs.

6. How does God give us "brothers and sisters and mothers and children" when we put Him first and follow Him?

7. How important is it to remember that the promise in Mark 10:29-30 includes "with persecutions, and in the age to come eternal life"?

8. Should the omnipresence of God (He is always with us and knows everything about us) strike fear or confidence in us?

9. Why should we not fear what man can do to us? What should we fear instead?

For Discussion

1. Although the devil does not have coercive powers, what powers does he have? What agencies does he sometimes use in the exercise of those powers?

2. God has coercive powers, but He has chosen never to use them in violation of our free moral natures. What agencies does He use to entice us to love Him and do His will?

3. What are some illustrations of the saying "All of Satan's apples have worms"?

4. What is the difference between pagans seeking after material things and Christians providing for themselves and their families?

7

PROVIDENCE
and Government

As Christians comment on the world scene – usually noting the decline of morality, the loss of respect for Christianity and the Bible in America, and the rising Muslim menace worldwide – we often say, "Remember, God is in control." That is certainly true. The Bible affirms it. However, it is important to examine Scripture and ask, "What does it mean to say, 'God is in control?'" and "To what extent does God involve Himself in the affairs of earthly kingdoms and their rulers?"

Three basic principles of God's dealings with His creation are applicable to these questions. (1) God made us freewill creatures, able to obey Him or rebel against Him. He does not violate mankind's free will. (2) Although human beings can act in sinful ways contrary to the expressed moral will of God, they cannot thwart God's ultimate will. (3) Choices that go contrary to God's expressed moral will carry consequences. God is not mocked. Whatever people sow, they will also reap (Galatians 6:7). That includes kings, presidents and the nations that follow them. Those who sow to the flesh by rebelling against God reap disaster and corruption (v. 8). The wise man's words are still true: "Righteousness exalts a nation, but sin is a reproach to any people" (Proverbs 14:34).

Nations in Charge

The inspired apostle commanded Christians concerning governmental rulers, "Let every person be subject to the governing authorities" (Romans 13:1). Then, he affirmed:

> For there is no authority except from God, and those that exist have been instituted by God. Therefore whoever resists the authorities resists what God has appointed, and those who resist will incur judgment. For rulers are not a terror to good conduct, but to bad. Would you have no fear of the one who is in authority? Then do what is good, and you will receive his approval, for he is God's servant for your good. But if you do wrong, be afraid, for he does not bear the sword in vain. For he is the servant of God, an avenger who carries out God's wrath on the wrongdoer. (vv. 1-4)

Although God may, on occasion, providentially influence who becomes a ruler in a particular instance, Romans 13 probably means, more generally, that God has ordained there should be earthly rulers rather than that He Himself appoints particular rulers. And although Romans 13 expresses a truth concerning rulers, it does not express the whole truth. Rulers sometimes forbid what Jesus has commanded and may command what the Lord forbids. In such cases, we learn from the example of the apostles Peter and John: "We must obey God rather than men" (Acts 5:29).

The prophet Habakkuk wrestled with this theme. He marveled that God allowed His people Israel to continue being so wicked so long. He asked: "O LORD, how long shall I cry for help, and you will not hear? Or cry to you 'Violence!' and you will not save?" (Habakkuk 1:2). Habakkuk then complained:

> Why do you make me see iniquity, and why do you idly look at wrong? Destruction and violence are before me; strife and contention arise. So the law is paralyzed, and justice never goes forth. For the wicked surround the righteous; so justice goes forth perverted. (vv. 3-4)

God responded to the prophet by saying He would raise up the Chaldeans (Babylonians) and use them to punish His people for their sins.

> Look among the nations, and see; wonder and be astounded. For I am doing a work in your days that you would not believe if told. For behold, I am raising up the Chaldeans, that bitter and hasty nation, who march through the breadth of the earth, to seize dwellings not their own. (Habakkuk 1:5-6)

Clearly, He said, "I am doing a work in your days," and "I am raising up the Chaldeans."

That troubled Habakkuk even more: "You who are of purer eyes than to see evil and cannot look at wrong, why do you idly look at traitors and are silent when the wicked swallows up the man more righteous than he?" (Habakkuk 1:13). So God said He would then raise up another nation to punish Babylon for their sins (2:2-20).

At that point, Habakkuk gave up trying to make human sense of God's divine ways – as we all should do sometimes. Habakkuk said:

> Though the fig tree should not blossom, nor fruit be on the vines, the produce of the olive fail and the fields yield no food, the flock be cut off from the fold and there be no herd in the stalls, yet I will rejoice in the LORD; I will take joy in the God of my salvation. (3:17-18)

We must trust God, even when we do not understand what He is doing.

Assyria preceded Babylon as a world empire, and just as God used Babylon to punish Judah, He used Assyria to punish the northern kingdom of Israel. The Lord called Assyria "the rod of my anger," saying, "Against a godless nation I send him, and against the people of my wrath I command him" (Isaiah 10:4-6). That naturally raises the same question Habakkuk asked: How could Assyria have been used to punish Israel when Assyria was guilty of even greater evil and violence than Israel?

Part of the answer is that God used Babylon to punish Assyria and then used the Medes and Persians to punish Babylon. This truth is thus reaffirmed: Nations' actions contrary to God's expressed moral will, even when used to accomplish God's ultimate purposes, still carry consequences. What nations sow, they also reap.

In fulfillment of the prophecy "Why do the nations rage and the peoples plot in vain? The kings of the earth set themselves, and the rulers take counsel together, against the LORD and against his Anointed" (Psalm 2:1-2), Pilate (ruler) and Herod (king) conspired with the Romans (nations) and the Jews (peoples) to try to stop God from establishing His kingdom and enthroning His Son as King. God laughed at their puny efforts and set His Son as King anyway (cf. Psalm 2 as interpreted in Acts 4:24-28).

The Jewish leaders acted out of envy (Mark 15:10). Pilate acted out of political expediency, fearful of angering Caesar. Peter said the mob "crucified and killed [Jesus] by the hands of lawless men" (Acts 2:23). Although their motives were evil and their actions, wicked, what they did was "according to the definite plan and foreknowledge of God" (v. 23). Their sinful actions accomplished God's ultimate plan to offer His Son for the sins of the world.

As previously noted, although human beings, including kings and presidents, can act in sinful ways contrary to the expressed moral will of God, they cannot prevent God's ultimate will from being accomplished. They may even unwittingly assist in it.

Conquering of Nations

Besides using evil nations to punish the wickedness of other nations, God also moved nations to bring about the fulfillment of His benevolent promises. God promised Judah they would return to the land from which they were exiled and their beloved Jerusalem and the temple of God would be rebuilt. Isaiah promised – amazingly even before the Babylonians had come to power – that the Medes and Persians would conquer Babylon (Isaiah 13) and the Persian King Cyrus (Isaiah identified him by his name centuries before he was born) would let the captive peoples go home. God called Cyrus "my shepherd" (44:28) and my "anointed" (45:1, same word as Hebrew "Messiah" and Greek "Christ"), promising " 'he shall fulfill all my purpose'; saying of Jerusalem, 'She shall be built,' and of the temple, 'Your foundation shall be laid' " (44:28).

The inspired chronicler of Judah, Isaiah, also gave God credit for Cyrus' decree:

> Now in the first year of Cyrus king of Persia, that the word of the LORD by the mouth of Jeremiah might be fulfilled, the LORD stirred up the spirit of Cyrus king of Persia, so that he made a proclamation throughout all his kingdom and also put it in writing: "Thus says Cyrus king of Persia, 'The LORD, the God of heaven, has given me all the kingdoms of the earth, and he has charged me to build him a house at Jerusalem, which is in Judah. Whoever is among you of all his people, may the LORD his God be with him. Let him go up.'" (2 Chronicles 36:22-23)

Although God was using Nebuchadnezzar and his Babylonian empire to punish His people with 70 years of captivity, Nebuchadnezzar became puffed up with pride. God humiliated him by forcing him to eat grass like a beast of the field "until [he knew] that the Most High rules the kingdom of men and gives it to whom he will" (Daniel 4:32). The lesson learned by Nebuchadnezzar affirms the thesis of this chapter: God is in control. It does not, however, answer all of the questions about how and when.

When God did things by miracles, they were "signs" that proved the persons through whom God worked them were His spokespersons. Their words were true, and their commandments were from God (John 3:2). His working in providence, however, as Paul noted in Philemon 15-16, is only "perhaps" when viewed from a human standpoint. Miracles are clearly from God. Providence is always "perhaps," except when God in Scripture tells us He is working behind the scenes.

Powerful nations built empires by conquering neighboring nations. Often that was not very difficult. The greater difficulty lay in keeping conquered nations in submission and paying tribute while the empire builder was off conquering other nations. Assyria and Babylon used terror to accomplish that.

If a conquered nation rebelled, its cities were completely destroyed. The people who survived the battle were uprooted and scattered among other nations. It has been said the Assyrians even contaminated a nation's agricultural fields so that nothing could grow. They thought making rebellion so costly would discourage others from trying. But their reign was so brutal and their demand for tribute so high that the example of terror was not enough. Nations kept rebelling anyway until finally one prevailed and became the next world empire.

The Persians decided to try a different method. They allowed the peoples that Babylon had driven into exile to go back to their homelands and rebuild their cities and temples. They even provided some monetary assistance, and although the captive peoples were still under Persian domination, they ruled them less brutally. Some might argue that providence had nothing to do with the Jews being allowed to go back to their land because the Persians let all of the captive peoples return home. We are not left to wonder, however, whether God's providential care for His people was at work in this case. God promised the Jews they would return, and He described Cyrus centuries earlier as His "anointed" to accomplish the return (Isaiah 45:1). God told us in Scripture He was working in this instance.

Choices Carry Consequences

What do we learn from this that is applicable to our time and circumstances? One certainly relevant lesson is "Righteousness exalts a nation, but sin is a reproach to any people" (Proverbs 14:34). "If the foundations are destroyed, what can the righteous do?" the psalmist asked (Psalm 11:3). In the rest of the psalm, he answered his own question: Keep right on being righteous, doing righteous deeds.

Why did God destroy Sodom? One obvious answer from the Genesis account is that they were given over to the practice of homosexuality (Genesis 19). Ezekiel added additional reasons: "Behold, this was the guilt of your sister Sodom: she and her daughters had pride, excess of food, and prosperous ease, but did not aid the poor and needy" (Ezekiel 16:49). Another obvious and important answer to the question, however, is that Sodom was destroyed because there were not 10 righteous people to be found within its walls. Abraham negotiated with God until God agreed not to destroy Sodom if 10 righteous people could be found there. God was still agreeing when

Abraham stopped asking, but 10 righteous people were not to be found (Genesis 18).

God may decide that America has become so wicked it needs to be punished. More than one gospel preacher has said, "If God does not punish America, He will have to apologize to Sodom and Gomorrah." While it does seem strange that God might use communist Russia or erratic, terroristic Iran to do so, it is no stranger than Him using Assyria and Babylon to punish Israel and Judah. Jesus said:

> And you, Capernaum, will you be exalted to heaven? You will be brought down to Hades. For if the mighty works done in you had been done in Sodom, it would have remained until this day. But I tell you that it will be more tolerable on the day of judgment for the land of Sodom than for you. (Matthew 11:23-24)

America has not had miracles performed in its boundaries as Capernaum did, but it does have an abundance of Bibles – the God-breathed, Holy Spirit–confirmed Word of God. It has the message of the crucified Christ – who said, "And I, when I am lifted up from the earth, will draw all people to myself" (John 12:32) – proclaimed everywhere. Abraham said that those who will not listen to Scripture will not believe if someone is risen from the dead (Luke 16:31). Jesus Christ has risen from the dead, yet many do not believe.

God hinted to Jeremiah that one righteous man might be enough to save Jerusalem: "Run to and fro through the streets of Jerusalem, look and take note! Search her squares to see if you can find a man, one who does justice and seeks truth, that I may pardon her" (Jeremiah 5:1). The Greek cynical philosopher Diogenes scoured Athens, holding up his lantern, looking in vain for an honest man.

If God were thinking about destroying America, what might He look for to cause Him to change His mind? Would He look for 10 righteous people or maybe 10,000? Would He find them? Would there be enough?

The single most powerful thing any one person can do for the preservation of his or her country and civilization is to be a faithful Christian and "walk in a manner worthy of the calling to which you have been called, with all humility and gentleness, with patience, bearing with one another in love" (Ephesians 4:1-2). That is how we become "the salt of the earth" (Matthew 5:13), and it is salt that saves and preserves.

Questions

1. Name three basic principles concerning God's dealings with humans that are also applicable in His dealings with nations and their rulers.

2. What are we to do when governmental authorities contradict God, either commanding us to do something God has forbidden or forbidding us from doing something God has commanded?

3. Why did the prophet Habakkuk cry out to God, "How long?"

4. What did God tell Habakkuk He was about to do?

5. How did God remain just when the nation He used to punish His people was even more wicked than His people?

6. Which nation did God call "the rod of [His] anger"?

7. Who did God name as His "anointed" in Isaiah 45:1?

8. What did Nebuchadnezzar learn from eating grass like a beast of the field that serves as a thesis statement for this chapter?

9. If the foundations are destroyed, what can the righteous do?

For Discussion

1. Does God always personally pick every president, king, emperor, governor, mayor, etc., in the world? Does He ever?

2. What is your reaction to the statement "If God does not punish America, He will have to apologize to Sodom and Gomorrah"?

3. How does Psalm 2, as interpreted in Acts 4:24-28, confirm that human rulers cannot thwart God's ultimate will? According to this passage, when did God establish His promised kingdom?

4. When nations and rulers go awry, we often comfort one another by saying, "Remember, God is in control." What biblical incidents and precepts qualify that statement? What questions does it leave unanswered?

5. What is the single most important thing a Christian can do to preserve his or her civilization and/or nation?

8

"THE LORD
Will Provide"

A mountain named Moriah was called *Yahweh-Jireh* by Abraham, an expression meaning "the LORD will provide" (Genesis 22:14). The incident leading up to that designation should not be overlooked in a study of the providence of God.

The Promise of a Son

God promised Abram, as he was called when we first read about him, that he would be the father of "a great nation" (Genesis 12:2). His descendants, God said, would be in number as "the dust of the earth" (13:16). Later promises were made also, but none of them were to be realized by Abram personally. Every promise was to be fulfilled in his descendants. Yet Abram was childless and old. He had no descendants and, from a physical standpoint, no prospects that he would ever have any.

At one point, Abram assumed God would fulfill these promises through Eliezer, his chief servant or steward, by recognizing him as Abram's heir (Genesis 15:2). That was a way estates of wealthy men who had no children were handled at that time, according to information found in the Nuzi tablets.[1] God told him no, not that way. "Your very own son shall be your heir," He said, and He promised Abram his descendants would be in number as the stars in the sky (vv. 4-5).

So Sarai and Abram decided to take matters into their own hands. Sarai had an Egyptian personal servant named Hagar. The laws of inheritance at that time, again according to the Nuzi tablets, provided for a son of the estate owner and a maidservant of his wife to be elevated to the position of heir of the estate if the estate owner so decreed. Sarai sent her maid in to Abram, and thus, Ishmael was born. But that was Abram and Sarai's scheme. It was not God's provision.

The Lord appeared again to Abram to reaffirm His covenant with him. Abram was 99 years old, and Sarai was 90. God changed their names from Abram ("exalted father") to Abraham ("father of a multitude") and from Sarai (the meaning of which is uncertain) to Sarah ("princess"). And the Lord said: "I will give you a son by her. I will bless her, and she shall become nations" (Genesis 17:1, 5, 15-17). God said this promised son of Sarah and Abraham was to be named Isaac and explicitly promised that Isaac would be the one with whom He would establish His covenant, the one through whom His promises to Abraham would be kept (v. 19).

Both Abraham and Sarah laughed at the idea that a man and woman so old, especially a woman who had passed the age of childbearing, could bear a child (cf. Genesis 17:17; 18:12). But God assured them it would happen, reminding them that nothing is too difficult for the Lord. Ultimately,

> the LORD visited Sarah as he had said, and the LORD did to Sarah as he had promised. And Sarah conceived and bore Abraham a son in his old age at the time of which God had spoken to him. Abraham called the name of his son who was born to him, whom Sarah bore him, Isaac. (21:1-3)

Then God specifically promised again, "Through Isaac shall your offspring be named" (Genesis 21:12).

Abraham's Example of Faith

It was "after these things God tested Abraham" (Genesis 22:1). The Lord told him, "Take your son, your only son Isaac, whom you love," and offer him as a burnt offering (v. 2). Isaac, as we have seen, was not Abraham's "only son" in the flesh. Hagar had borne him Ishmael. But Isaac was the only son of Sarah and Abraham. More to the point, he was the only son of promise. He was the son of whom God had said, "Through Isaac shall your offspring be named" (21:12). For God's promises to prove true, Isaac had to live and have children. Abraham understood that, and that is an essential key to understanding God's testing of Abraham's faith.

In nearly every extensive discussion of faith found in the New Testament, Abraham is used as an example of true faith. It was characteristic of Abraham to respond vigorously and immediately when called upon to demonstrate his faith. We first meet Abram, as he was then called, in Haran, where God told him: "Go from your country and your kindred and your father's house to the land that I will show you. And I will make of you a great nation, and I will bless you and make your name great, so that you will be a blessing" (Genesis 12:1-2). What was Abram's response? He "went, as the LORD had told him, and Lot went with him. Abram was seventy-five years old when he departed from Haran" (v. 4).

Later on, God's command was much more difficult: "Take your son, your only son Isaac, whom you love, and go to the land of Moriah, and offer him there as a burnt offering on one of the mountains of which I shall tell you" (Genesis 22:2). Although God's command seemed contrary to His promises, faithful Abraham did not hesitate. He understood God's commands were not to be questioned, but obeyed. "So Abraham rose early in the morning, saddled his donkey, and took two of his young men with him, and his son Isaac. And he cut the wood for the burnt offering and arose and went to the place of which God had told him" (v. 3).

The rest of the story is well-known. The angel of the Lord stayed Abraham's hand as he was about to slay Isaac, showing him a ram instead, and Abraham offered the ram on the altar to God.

Two phrases from the Genesis account of this incident point to Abraham's expectation. When Abraham, Isaac and Abraham's servants neared the mountain where God had said the sacrifice was to be offered, Abraham told the young men to stay with the donkey he had ridden. Then he said, "I and the boy will go over there and worship and come again to you" (Genesis 22:5). "I and the boy will … come again to you" was a prophetic statement. That Abraham stated it that way shows his expectation that the Lord would provide a way for His promises to be kept even as His seemingly contrary commandment was obeyed.

As Abraham and Isaac approached the place where the sacrifice was to be offered, Isaac said, "Behold, the fire and the wood, but where is the lamb for a burnt offering?" (Genesis 22:7). Abraham replied, "God will provide for himself the lamb for a burnt offering, my son" (v. 8). Once again, Abraham spoke – perhaps not fully understanding what he had said, certainly not knowing what or how the Lord would provide – with an expectation of divine provision that would enable Isaac to survive. The Lord did provide. No sooner did the angel stop Abraham from sacrificing his son than Abraham saw a ram with his horns tangled in underbrush. He offered that ram in sacrifice to the Lord.

It did not require a miracle for a ram to be caught, tangled in a thicket. Such things happen. But for it to have happened at that precise time makes it manifestly an act of God – God's providence, in fact. Significantly, after this incident, Abraham named that place *Yahweh-Jireh* or "the LORD will provide" (Genesis 22:14).

The writer of Hebrews said:

> By faith Abraham, when he was tested, offered up Isaac, and he who had received the promises was in the act of offering up his only son, of whom it was said, "Through Isaac shall your offspring be named." He considered that God was able even to raise him from the dead, from which, figuratively speaking, he did receive him back. (11:17-19)

This incident does indeed show Abraham's faith. He passed the test. He had confidence enough in God to do what God had said, even though it appeared contrary to the promises God had made. Abraham knew God would provide and would keep His promises even if it required raising Isaac from the dead.

Father of the Faithful

Abraham is called "the father of all those who believe" (Romans 4:11) or "the father of the faithful." The Bible uses him as an example of the kind of faith that blesses and saves virtually every time faith is illustrated. When Abraham accepted God's word that He would give him and Sarah a son, even though it would take a miracle for them to conceive, Scripture says, "And he believed the LORD, and he counted it to him as righteousness" (Genesis 15:6).

When James wanted to demonstrate that faith without works is dead, he wrote:

> Was not Abraham our father justified by works when he offered up his son Isaac on the altar? You see that faith was active along with his works, and faith was completed by his works, and the Scripture was fulfilled that says, "Abraham believed God, and it was counted to him as righteousness." (James 2:20-23)

Abraham's faith was not a dead or useless faith. It was a living and saving faith. As an illustration that Abraham's was a faith that would act, James used the fact that Abraham had offered up the very son through whom the promises of God were to be fulfilled.

Our children need to know that the God we serve does not ask for them to be put to death on an altar of sacrifice. They also need to know that we have the kind of faith Abraham had if we are to be an heir by faith to the promises God made to Abraham. Like Abraham, let us unwaveringly believe God. He will count our faith as righteousness, and He will provide.

Questions

1. What does *Yahweh-Jireh* mean?

2. When Abraham was told by God to leave his kinsmen and homeland and go to a place God would show him, what was his first reaction?

3. How many children did Abraham have when God promised to make him "a great nation" in Genesis 12:2?

4. Virtually every promise God made to Abraham was to be fulfilled through whom?

5. What do the names "Abraham" and "Sarah" mean?

6. When God told Abraham to sacrifice his son Isaac, what was He testing?

7. What two things did Abraham say in the Genesis account that show he expected to come back from the mountain with Isaac alive?

8. To Isaac's question "Where is the lamb for a burnt offering?", Abraham responded, "God will provide." What and how did God provide?

For Discussion

1. Although Abraham is frequently used in the Bible as an example of strong, obedient faith, does the arrangement between him and Sarah and Hagar, resulting in Ishmael, indicate a weakness of faith at that point?

2. God's original plan for marriage was one man for one woman for life. Throughout the Old Testament, there were other arrangements that violated that ideal (Matthew 19:8). However, deviations from that plan often did not work out very well. How does the story of Abraham, Sarah and Hagar illustrate that?

3. The angel of the Lord stopped Abraham's hand from killing Isaac and said, "Do not lay your hand on the boy or do anything to him, for now I know that you fear God, seeing you have not withheld your son, your only son, from me" (Genesis 22:12). If God already knew what Abraham would do before He tested him, for whose benefit, do you think, was the test done?

4. Abraham is used several times as an example of the kind of faith that saves. What kind of faith is that? What does it save from?

9

THE LIVES OF
Joseph and Esther

T wo times God's people in the Old Testament were threatened with extinction: once by famine in the days of the patriarchs and once by a determined enemy close to the emperor who was in control of the world at the time. Both times they were saved – not by miraculous means as when God, on another occasion, killed 185,000 enemy soldiers in one night, but by means best described as providential.

Providence in Joseph's Journey

In the first instance, God used Joseph, the favorite son of Jacob.

Some miracles were involved. Joseph's prophetic dreams and his ability to interpret the prophetic dreams of others were miraculous. But mostly the Israelites' salvation involved the kind of "more than coincidental" things that imply providence. In this case, we go beyond "perhaps" to certainty because Scripture tells us God worked behind the scenes to make things happen. Joseph told his brothers, "As for you, you meant evil against me, but God meant it for good, to bring it about that many people should be kept alive, as they are today" (Genesis 50:20).

To trace the hand of God as He providentially saved the people of God from famine, we will start at the end of Joseph's story. Joseph was second in command only to Pharaoh in Egypt and was in charge of vast storehouses of grain in a time of severe, widespread famine – a position he managed to obtain after correctly interpreting Pharaoh's dreams, which had predicted the famine.

He would not have been available to interpret Pharaoh's dreams had the butler, whose favorable dream Joseph had interpreted earlier, not forgotten to tell Pharaoh about Joseph as soon as he got out of prison as he had intended to do. But having had forgotten, when Pharaoh had his dreams that no one could satisfactorily interpret, the butler then remembered Joseph and told Pharaoh.

However, if Joseph had not been in prison, where he correctly interpreted the dreams of the butler and the baker, the butler would not have known to recommend him to Pharaoh. As one considers it, it is quite unusual that the butler, although in prison presumably for something serious, was reestablished as Pharaoh's butler after he was released. But if he had not been, he would not have had the opportunity to tell Pharaoh of Joseph, who had correctly interpreted his dream.

Joseph, however, would not have been in prison had Potiphar's wife not lied about him, accusing him of trying to rape her when, in reality, it was she who had tried unsuccessfully to seduce Joseph. It is a wonder that Potiphar did not have Joseph put to death. As owner of a slave, he certainly had that power, and the circumstances reported to him by his wife, in many instances, would have brought about that conclusion. One wonders, then, whether Potiphar had more faith in Joseph than in his wife. The overall effect of Joseph's character and integrity, which had so impressed Potiphar that he made Joseph his chief steward, makes that a likely scenario. Of course, he had to show some credence to his wife for the sake of appearances; all of that makes it understandable that Potiphar had Joseph put in prison rather than executing him immediately.

The chain of interesting, providential circumstances is still not complete. Joseph would not have even been in Egypt had his brothers not sold him into slavery. That was brought about by the favoritism shown to Joseph by his father, which was aggravated no doubt by Joseph's recounting of his dreams that implied his superiority. And the brothers' plan would not have worked out had the traders been just a few minutes later in passing, for Reuben had planned to come by and free Joseph.

A whole set of remarkable circumstances, some would say coincidences – some good, some related to the integrity of Joseph, some related to the evil of others – all worked together to put Joseph in position to save his family from famine.

During all this time, what was Joseph thinking? He thought at first that as soon as his father learned he had been sold into Egypt, he would come get him. After many months when no one came, he began to think no one cared. He married and named his first son Manasseh, which means "forgetfulness," saying, "God has made me forget all my hardship and all my father's house" (Genesis 41:51).

Only later, after overhearing conversations between his brothers (which they did not expect Joseph to understand), did he learn that his father had thought him dead all these years and that the brothers who had so crassly sold him into slavery were now willing to be slaves themselves rather than go back home without Benjamin. It was then that Joseph called for all of his family to come to Egypt, where, because of his wise leadership, there was plenty of food.

God had a hand in these "coincidences," overruling the jealous brothers' intent and using even their sinfulness to accomplish His purposes. Joseph told his brothers, "As for you, you meant evil against me, but God meant it for good, to bring it about that many people should be kept alive, as they are today" (Genesis 50:20). The providence of God worked for the good of God's people in the life of Joseph.

Providence in Esther's Rise to Royalty

The second time God's people in the Old Testament were threatened with extinction, they were in exile. Some had returned to rebuild Jerusalem and the temple, but many were still scattered throughout the Persian Empire. They were scheduled to be wiped out because of the jealousy and pride of a vicious egomaniac named Haman, who happened to have the ear of the Persian king. Their peril was exacerbated by the fact that a law of the Medes and Persians, once decreed, could not be later rescinded.

God chose, in this instance, a devout and beautiful Jewish maiden named Esther as the instrument of His providence. Interestingly, the book of Esther, which contains this crucial incident in the history of God's people, is the only book in the Bible, Old or New Testament, that does not contain the name of God. It records no miracle. It has no explicit reference to an action of God. However, the work of God's hand is evident nonetheless.

The name of the Persian king to the Greeks was Xerxes and to the Jews, Ahasuerus. Near Eastern history remembers him as the king who launched an invasion of Greece and fought a famous battle with 300 Spartans at Thermopylae. As the book of Esther opens, Ahasuerus was presiding over a lavish banquet given for the political and military notables in the Medo-Persian Empire. Queen Vashti was entertaining the women in a similar banquet. "On the seventh day, when the heart of the king was merry with wine," he commanded Queen Vashti to be brought to the banquet "in order to show the peoples and the princes her beauty, for she was lovely to look at" (Esther 1:10-11). Vashti, showing commendable modesty, refused the king's command.

Some punitive response to Vashti's refusal to come at the king's bidding would have to be made, it was decided, lest all of the wives throughout the empire followed Vashti's example and refused the commands of their husbands. It might be supposed that Ahasuerus did not have Vashti put to death because he realized his command to her was itself unseemly and should not have been given. What the king did, however, was remove Vashti from being queen and begin the search for a replacement (Esther 1).

Vashti's modesty, her refusal to parade her beauty before the drunken nobles and governors of the provinces, is the first link in a chain of events that would ultimately save the Jews from extinction.

A Jew by the name of Mordecai had been among the nobles and princes who were taken into exile in Babylon at the same time as Daniel and his three friends (Esther 2:6; Daniel 1:2-4). Mordecai had a beautiful young cousin named Esther, whom he had adopted as his daughter. Esther was chosen by Ahasuerus to be queen. Link two in the chain.

A plot by two of Ahasuerus' servants to kill the king became known to Mordecai; Mordecai told Esther, and Esther told Ahasuerus. The plotters were executed, and the event was entered into the chronicles of the kingdom. Link three.

Enter Haman. Haman had ingratiated himself with King Ahasuerus and had become the king's favorite. He was promoted above the other princes and nobles so that they were all commanded to bow down and pay homage to Haman whenever he passed. Mordecai would not bow.

"And when Haman saw that Mordecai did not bow down or pay homage to him, Haman was filled with fury" (Esther 3:5).

Knowing that Mordecai was a Jew, Haman determined to have not just Mordecai but all Jews throughout the kingdom of the Medes and Persians put to death. He persuaded the king, with lies and bribery, to issue a decree that on a specified day all Jews were to be killed and their goods, confiscated (Esther 3:13).

Mordecai refusing to bow continued to aggravate Haman. Later, after many honors had been heaped on Haman, so he thought, Haman told his wife, "Yet all this is worth nothing to me, so long as I see Mordecai the Jew sitting at the king's gate" (Esther 5:13). His wife then told him to build a gallows and have Mordecai hanged on it the next day.

Returning to the chain of events that resulted in the rescue of the Jews from annihilation, while Haman was having the gallows built on which to hang Mordecai, the king had a sleepless night. He decided to pass the night by reading from the chronicles of his kingdom. He read of the plot to put him to death, of Mordecai's learning about the plot and reporting it, and of the plot thereby being thwarted. He inquired, "What honor or distinction has been bestowed on Mordecai for this?" (Esther 6:3).

Learning that nothing had been done, he determined to rectify that. "Who is in the court?" the king asked. "The king's young men told him, 'Haman is there, standing in the court' " (Esther 6:5-6). Haman had come to request permission to hang Mordecai on the gallows he had built. He was brought in, and the king asked him, "What should be done to the man whom the king delights to honor?" (v. 6). Haman could not imagine that the king wanted to honor anyone more than himself, so he said:

> For the man whom the king delights to honor, let royal
> robes be brought, which the king has worn, and the horse
> that the king has ridden, and on whose head a royal crown
> is set. And let the robes and the horse be handed over to
> one of the king's most noble officials. Let them dress the
> man whom the king delights to honor, and let them lead
> him on the horse through the square of the city, proclaim-
> ing before him: "Thus shall it be done to the man whom
> the king delights to honor." Then the king said to Haman,

"Hurry; take the robes and the horse, as you have said, and do so to Mordecai the Jew who sits at the king's gate. Leave out nothing that you have mentioned." (Esther 6:7-10)

Although Mordecai's moment of honor mortified Haman, it did nothing to thwart Haman's plan to annihilate Mordecai and his people. So Mordecai approached Esther, asking her to go before the king and plead their case. However, the king of the Medes and Persians did not want to be bothered with unwanted visitors. When anyone came to see him uninvited, if the king did not hold out his scepter to him, the uninvited guest was to be immediately killed. Even as his wife, Esther was subject to the same restriction if she approached the king uninvited.

Yet, at great risk to herself, Esther appeared before the king. When Ahasuerus extended his scepter to her, she invited him and Haman to attend a banquet. At the feast, the king asked Esther what she desired of him. He knew, of course, that she had not risked her life just to invite him to dinner, but at that point, all she would ask was that the two of them return for another feast the next day.

There, Esther revealed her request. A plot had been concocted to kill her and all of her people throughout the empire. Wicked Haman was responsible for the plot, and she pleaded for the life of herself and her people. The king left the room in anger; Haman was terrified and threw himself on the couch where Esther was reclining to plead for his life. The king came back in the room and thought Haman was assaulting the queen in the king's very presence and in his own house. Haman was immediately hanged on the gallows that he had prepared for Mordecai.

Although the king's order concerning the Jews could not be revoked, a new order was sent out under the king's seal allowing and encouraging the Jews to defend themselves on the day when they were supposed to be annihilated. That let the kingdom know where the king's allegiance now lay; instead of the Jews, the enemies of the Jews suffered annihilation. That day was declared a feast day, and it is celebrated by the Jewish people as the Feast of Purim to this day.

Despite the fact that no mention of God or of any explicit act of God is mentioned in the book of Esther, there are inspired indications that God's providential hand was at work. When Mordecai was sending word to Esther, pleading with her to intervene, he sent this word:

> Do not think to yourself that in the king's palace you will escape any more than all the other Jews. For if you keep silent at this time, relief and deliverance will rise for the Jews from another place, but you and your father's house will perish. And who knows whether you have not come to the kingdom for such a time as this? (Esther 4:13-14)

Mordecai was aware of the promises God had made to the Jews since the time of Abraham and of the steadfast love of God that ensured His promises would be kept. Therefore, he was confident in saying, "If you keep silent at this time, relief and deliverance will rise for the Jews from another place" (Esther 4:14). Somehow, in God's gracious providence, the Jews would be spared to fulfill their role and bless all the families of the world through the promised Messiah. Mordecai's words to Esther also suggest it would be through her that God would provide a rescue: "And who knows whether you have not come to the kingdom for such a time as this?" (v. 14).

God has, on occasion, saved His people in miraculous ways. He saved them from the malevolent jealousy of Haman and his decree to kill all the Jews, but this time is was not by an angel of the Lord killing 185,000 enemy soldiers or by the walls of a city falling down flat. It was by a string of remarkable "coincidences" that we can say were not just coincidental but providential. As Mordecai said, "relief and deliverance will rise for the Jews" (Esther 4:14) – by a king who, because he could not sleep, read of a forgotten favor and by a brave and virtuous queen who risked her life to plead for the lives of her people.

A poem by James Russell Lowell, often quoted by W.B. West as expressing the theme of Revelation, is appropriate here as well: "Truth forever on the scaffold, Wrong forever on the throne, – / Yet that scaffold sways the future, and, behind the dim unknown, / Standeth God within the shadow, keeping watch above his own."

God is still keeping watch above His own. Any one of us at any time could be in a situation that would call for faithful, effective action on our parts to bring about God's will for His church. Who knows whether we may have come to the kingdom for just such a time as that? Let us be perceptive and ready.

Questions

1. How did it happen that, when Pharaoh had some dreams no one could interpret, Joseph was called to interpret them?

2. Precisely because Joseph was a godly and virtuous young man, he wound up in prison. How did that happen?

3. What might have happened if Reuben's plan to rescue Joseph from the pit had worked out?

4. Why did Joseph name his first son Manasseh?

5. In Joseph's story, what was God saving the lives of His people from?

6. What book of the Bible does not make any direct reference to God?

7. What caused Haman to hate the Jews? What did he do because of his hatred?

8. What did Mordecai do that caused his name to be written in the chronicles of the king?

9. What Jewish feast still celebrates the day the Jews were supposed to be annihilated but ended up killing many of their enemies instead?

10. Why was Mordecai so certain that, if Esther did not act to save her people, relief and deliverance would come for the Jews from another place (Esther 4:14)?

For Discussion

1. What part did the integrity of Joseph play in the scenarios that ended up with him as a ruler in Egypt?

2. What words of Mordecai to Esther point to the likelihood of providence playing a part in the salvation of the Jews in Persia? Does the fact that God could have delivered the Jews another way negate the importance of Esther's decision to confront the king?

3. What do you learn from Joseph's and Esther's stories about sacrificing self for the greater good of God's people?

10

PROVIDENCE
and Discipline

The epistle to the Hebrews was addressed to Jewish Christians who were evidently giving serious consideration to turning away from Christ and returning to the worship of God under the Mosaic covenant. Therefore, the writer in this "word of exhortation" (Hebrews 13:22) contrasted every aspect of the New Covenant of Christ with the corresponding aspect of the Covenant of Moses and showed the new to be better and superior in every way.

As the book of Acts shows, Jewish Christians were persecuted vigorously by the Jews, who rejected Jesus. Such persecution may have at least contributed to the desire of some Jewish Christians to return to the laws of Moses. The Christians to whom Hebrews was addressed had certainly suffered persecution:

> But recall the former days when, after you were enlightened, you endured a hard struggle with sufferings, sometimes being publicly exposed to reproach and affliction, and sometimes being partners with those so treated. For you had compassion on those in prison, and you joyfully accepted the plundering of your property, since you knew

that you yourselves had a better possession and an abiding one. (Hebrews 10:32-34)

Some of their number were in prison as the epistle was being written (Hebrews 13:2). Addressing these concerns, the Hebrews writer said:

It is for discipline that you have to endure. God is treating you as sons. For what son is there whom his father does not discipline? If you are left without discipline, in which all have participated, then you are illegitimate children and not sons. Besides this, we have had earthly fathers who disciplined us and we respected them. Shall we not much more be subject to the Father of spirits and live? For they disciplined us for a short time as it seemed best to them, but he disciplines us for our good, that we may share his holiness. For the moment all discipline seems painful rather than pleasant, but later it yields the peaceful fruit of righteousness to those who have been trained by it. (12:3-11)

A number of questions are suggested by this reading: If unbelieving Jews were persecuting these Christians for being Christians, how was their persecution "discipline" from their Father God? For what was God chastising them? Is every instance of opposition in a Christian's life discipline from the Lord? Is every calamity in a Christian's experience a chastisement from God? These questions obviously cry out for consideration in any contemplation of the providence of God.

Persecution Brings Blessing

My wife often says that, if she could have, she would have protected our four children from every hardship, every disappointment and every case of mistreatment from others whether real or imagined. She wanted to make their lives always pleasant and enjoyable. She also says, however, that if she had been able to do that, she would have succeeded in making all four of them milquetoasts, unfit for worthwhile accomplishments.

In the same way that bodily exercise is necessary for physical strength, if our "spiritual muscles" are to grow, they must be exercised against opposition, temptation, trouble and persecution. Because persecution and trials result in growth, both James and Paul stated they are to be appreciated and joyfully received. "Count it all joy, my brothers, when you meet trials of various kinds, for you know that the testing of your faith produces steadfastness" (James 1:2-3). Paul added,

> Not only that, but we rejoice in our sufferings, knowing that suffering produces endurance, and endurance produces character, and character produces hope, and hope does not put us to shame, because God's love has been poured into our hearts through the Holy Spirit who has been given to us. (Romans 5:3-5)

One of the psalmists said: "Before I was afflicted I went astray, but now I keep your word. ... It is good for me that I was afflicted, that I might learn your statutes" (Psalm 119:67, 71).

To be persecuted for doing right is to be among the truly blessed.

> Blessed are those who are persecuted for righteousness' sake, for theirs is the kingdom of heaven. Blessed are you when others revile you and persecute you and utter all kinds of evil against you falsely on my account. Rejoice and be glad, for your reward is great in heaven, for so they persecuted the prophets who were before you. (Matthew 5:10-12)

In addition to the blessings and efficacy of persecution, Scripture also reminds us of its inevitability for the faithful: "Indeed, all who desire to live a godly life in Christ Jesus will be persecuted" (2 Timothy 3:12). Jesus Himself said: "Remember the word that I said to you: 'A servant is not greater than his master.' If they persecuted me, they will also persecute you. If they kept my word, they will also keep yours" (John 15:20).

Historians have noted that Christianity has thrived in times of persecution. An early Christian writer famously noted: "That's why you can't just exterminate us; the more you kill the more we are. The blood of the martyrs is the seed of the church." [1] Students of homiletics point out that opposition seems better for Christianity than governmental or societal approval. The kingdom grows more when it must struggle against opposition than when it finds easy acceptance and Christians are allowed to live affluent lifestyles.

The wise man that Scripture identifies as Agur recognized this phenomenon and suggested we pray: "Give me neither poverty nor riches; feed me with the food that is needful for me, lest I be full and deny you and say, 'Who is the LORD?' or lest I be poor and steal and profane the name of my God" (Proverbs 30:8-9).

None of that says, however, that persecution, or any chastisement, is pleasant while it continues. "For the moment all discipline seems painful rather than pleasant, but later it yields the peaceful fruit of righteousness to those who have been trained by it" (Hebrews 12:11). Looking to its results and appreciating its benefits help us to bear persecution, even to rejoice in it. Of Jesus, the Hebrews writer explained that "for the joy that was set before him [He] endured the cross, despising the shame, and is seated at the right hand of the throne of God" (v. 2). The "joy that was set before him" included the redemption of myriads of sinners for whom He was giving His life and His own prophesied exalted position at the right hand of God's throne.

Jesus despised the shame of the cross (Hebrews 12:2). That does not mean He hated it. To "despise" is to count as nothing. Shameful and painful as the cross was, the results He knew He was accomplishing made it of no account. When we are persecuted, we are to remember "the sufferings of this present time are not worth comparing with the glory that is to be revealed to us" (Romans 8:18).

Calamities Are Not Proof of Sinful Lifestyles

Moses – especially in Deuteronomy, though also in Psalms – frequently assured the people that obedience to God would bring long life and prosperity while laziness and sin would bring poverty and early death. While that was (and is) a general truth, it was not a universal rule.

Job's three friends, like many at that time, believed every calamity to be caused by specific sin and, despite Job's protestations to the contrary, persisted in telling him he needed to acknowledge whatever great transgression he was hiding. Readers of Job, however, being privy to the conversation between God and Satan that preceded Satan's attack on Job, know that Job had not committed any great sin. On the contrary, he was, by God's estimation, "a blameless and upright man, who fears God and turns away from evil" (Job 1:8). And "the rest of the story" is that God vindicated Job by telling Job's three miserable counselors that He would accept Job's prayers for them and forgive them.

The view that calamity is always punishment for sin was still prevalent in New Testament times. Jesus and His disciples saw a man blind from birth, "and his disciples asked him, 'Rabbi, who sinned, this man or his parents, that he was born blind?' " (John 9:2). It should have been obvious that the man himself could not have sinned before he was born, but the view that "sin brings calamity, and calamity proves sin" was so ingrained they believed it had to be either the man himself or his parents who had caused this terrible malady.

Yet Jesus answered, "It was not that this man sinned, or his parents, but that the works of God might be displayed in him" (John 9:3). "That the works of God might be displayed in him" is likely not a statement of the reason the man was born blind but a statement of an intended result of his blindness. Either way, Jesus unequivocally denied any necessary linkage between people's maladies and specific sins on their part.

Some sins do bring their own punishment. Constant drinking can result in cirrhosis of the liver. Sexual promiscuity can result in contracting a sexually transmitted disease (Romans 1:27). Drunk drivers often maim or kill themselves as well as innocent victims. Yet bodily ailments and other calamities do not, in themselves, indicate sin. Although the Hebrews writer referred to persecution as "discipline" (Hebrews 12:4-5), nothing in the Hebrews text suggests it was to be understood as punishment for specific sins. Rather, it was to be received as discipline from the Lord, which shows His approval of them as His legitimate children.

Discipline Signifies God's Approval

In his discussion of discipline, the Hebrews writer began by pointing his readers to Christ, saying, "Consider him who endured from sinners such hostility against himself, so that you may not grow weary or fainthearted" (Hebrews 12:3). Peter also pointed persecuted Christians to Christ, as an example of suffering for righteousness' sake:

> For what credit is it if, when you sin and are beaten for it, you endure? But if when you do good and suffer for it you

> endure, this is a gracious thing in the sight of God. For to this you have been called, because Christ also suffered for you, leaving you an example, so that you might follow in his steps. (1 Peter 2:20-21)

Jesus' suffering was certainly a sign of His approval by God. "Although he was a son, he learned obedience through what he suffered. And being made perfect, he became the source of eternal salvation to all who obey him" (Hebrews 5:8-9). God accepted Christ's suffering as a sufficient propitiation "for our sins, and not for ours only but also for the sins of the whole world" (1 John 2:2). Christ's suffering, however, went far beyond that of the recipients of the epistle to the Hebrews. He died, where they had "not yet resisted to the point of shedding your blood" (Hebrews 12:4).[2]

The writer quoted Solomon (Proverbs 3:1-12) as showing that discipline is a sign of acceptance and legitimate sonship in God's family. Then the Hebrews writer added that a father who has an illegitimate son — one who, therefore, will not bear the father's name — may not care how such a son is reared. On the other hand, a son who is a part of the father's family will carry on the father's name, so the father will care enough to discipline him and shape his conduct. Therefore, because the Jewish Christians were being persecuted and, thus, disciplined, the Hebrews writer said, "God is treating you as sons" (Hebrews 12:7). In light of this, we should accept tribulation not in self-pity or resentment but as discipline from a loving Father and as evidence He cares. We are His children.

The providence of God brings to mind God blessing us and providing for our needs. In Hebrews, however, persecution, imprisonment, the plundering of their goods, and even the threat of death were provisions God made for Jewish Christians. These were all for discipline, Scripture says. Discipline spurs our spiritual growth. By it we are blessed. By it we are claimed by God as His children.

God provides many blessings. He provides food, shelter and clothing; protection, comfort and constant companionship; answers to pleading prayers; a way of escape in times of temptation; and something good out of every calamity. He also provides discipline. "Count it all joy" (James 1:2).

Questions

1. What blessings come from persecutions, trials and other difficulties, regardless of what causes them?

2. How are our "spiritual muscles" exercised?

3. According to historians, what has often been the result of Christian persecution?

4. What should be our attitude toward affliction, trials and even persecution that we or our loved ones suffer? Why?

5. What did the Hebrews writer mean by saying Jesus despised the shame of the cross?

6. What did many ancient people believe about sin and personal calamity?

7. What did the Hebrews writer say persecution is a sign of?

8. How is Jesus our example in matters of suffering for righteousness' sake?

9. What is the difference in the way a father treats a child whom he acknowledges as his own versus one who is illegitimate and unclaimed?

10. God blesses us with good things. When those good things are persecutions and chastisement, how should we react to them?

For Discussion

1. When a Christian is persecuted for righteousness' sake, it is not a punishment for sin. In what sense, then, is it discipline from the Lord?

2. If God disciplines those whom He loves and if all who live godly lives will suffer persecution, what should we perhaps contemplate if our lives run too smoothly?

3. What Bible books and/or passages teach us that personal infirmities are not always caused by the sin of the person who suffers them?

PROVIDENCE
and the Holy Spirit

G od's Spirit dwells in every Christian. "Or do you not know that your body is a temple of the Holy Spirit within you, whom you have from God?" (1 Corinthians 6:19). He is given as a gift to all who obey God (Acts 5:32). The Spirit is God's down payment to us, reminding us of the surety that God will fulfill all of His promises. He is "the guarantee of our inheritance until we acquire possession of it" (Ephesians 1:14).

Does the Holy Spirit play a part in God's gracious providential care for His people? We have observed that we can believe confidently, based on God's promises in Scripture, that God is at work, providing for us. However, we are generally not able to say with certainty whether His providential hand has been directly involved in a specific instance. So also, while we can know through Scripture that the Spirit does do certain things, we will not always know how, when or whether He has worked in a specific instance.

The Myth of Feelings

Many think of the Holy Spirit and His work as being validated by something we feel. Feelings are subjective; the promises of God are objective and sure. Whether God is with us, whether He is hearing our prayers, and whether we are His children are not determined by how we feel. We can be discouraged and believe that our prayers are getting no higher than the ceiling, but God hears our prayers when we, as His faithful children, pray in faith in the name of Christ – regardless of whether we feel like He does. We can be on an emotional high and feel that the Spirit is filling the room, but if what we are doing is not pleasing to Him, our feelings will be deceiving.

Feelings do not determine what is true; feelings result from what we believe on other grounds to be true. A classic example of that fact is Jacob's overwhelming grief when he believed Joseph was dead. If feelings were proof of anything, Joseph would have been dead; but he was very much alive and in Egypt being prepared by God to save his father and brothers from famine. Jacob's grief was no less severe than it would have been had Joseph been dead; his grief was the result of his belief that Joseph was dead (Genesis 37:29-36).

Because truth is determined by God's Word, not by feelings, God's objective Word always trumps our subjective feelings.

The Indwelling Spirit

Many books are available in the self-help section of the bookstore or library, but the Bible is not one of them. Christianity is not just a self-help religion. God does not just forgive us at baptism and then leave us with nothing more than our personal resources and weak will power to meet His high expectations of discipleship. The scripture that says "Work out your own salvation with fear and trembling" adds the words "for it is God who works in you, both to will and to work for his good pleasure" (Philippians 2:12-13).

How does God work in us as we work out our own salvation? Who can say that he knows? Yet what Bible believer can deny that God does this? One way we are "strengthened with power" (Ephesians 3:16) is by Scripture. The Word of God's grace is able to build us up (Acts 20:32). The Christians in Ephesus, however, were also strengthened through God's indwelling Spirit, "through his Spirit in your inner being" (Ephesians 3:16). The power of God to do beyond all that we ask or think is "according to the power at work within us" (v. 20). As we live the Christian life, "it is no longer [we] who live, but Christ who lives in [us]" (Galatians 2:20).

"The prince of the power of the air" is "the spirit that now works in the sons of disobedience" (Ephesians 2:2), but John assured us, "Little children, you are from God and have overcome them, for he who is in you is greater than he who is in the world" (1 John 4:4). Some kind of divine assistance working in us is presupposed in those passages. It is not miraculous; there is no supernatural sign to confirm its reality. It is not revelatory; no God-breathed information comes from it. Some say the Spirit helps us to win the struggle we have with sin and to defeat temptation. Yet those who say this still succumb to sinful attitudes and actions, as we all do.

The passage that says most clearly that God's Spirit dwells in our fleshly bodies also shows that one of the purposes of the Spirit's indwelling is to motivate believers to give their bodies as instruments of holiness and to avoid sexual sin:

> Flee from sexual immorality. Every other sin a person commits is outside the body, but the sexually immoral person sins against his own body. Or do you not know that your body is a temple of the Holy Spirit within you, whom you have from God? You are not your own, for you were bought with a price. So glorify God in your body. (1 Corinthians 6:18-20)

If a Christian were tempted to have sex with someone other than his wife – or with anyone, if he were not married – and if he were conscious of Paul's teaching that his body is God's dwelling place, surely that would help dissuade him from dishonoring God's temple by desecrating it with sexual immorality. In another lengthy admonition in which the apostle gave a number of reasons why Christians should "abstain from sexual immorality," the fact of the Spirit's indwelling appears again: "For this is the will of God, your sanctification: that you abstain from sexual immorality; ... Therefore whoever disregards this, disregards not man but God, who gives his Holy Spirit to you" (1 Thessalonians 4:3, 8).

Some hoodlums who vandalize schools and homes might be more hesitant to vandalize a church building because of its connection to the sacred. Christians are here reminded that God's temple is not a building made with hands but the bodies of faithful Christians. He dwells in us. Therefore, we should glorify God in our bodies and not dishonor Him or His temple by using it for immorality.

Continual Cleansing From Sin

One significant thing the Spirit does in us was explained by Paul in Romans 7–8. Romans 7 records Paul's struggle with sin. Most Christians, probably all, are able to identify with Paul as he said:

> I do not understand my own actions. For I do not do what I want, but I do the very thing I hate. ... For I have the desire to do what is right, but not the ability to carry it out. For I do not do the good I want, but the evil I do not want is what I keep on doing. (vv. 15, 18-19)

He clearly evidenced in these expressions of his inner war with temptation that he was not content to sin. He was not willfully continuing in a sinful lifestyle. He hated his sins and was always sorry and penitent whenever he sinned. His mindset was clearly desirous of the things of the Spirit, not the things of the flesh (Romans 8:5).

A major theme in Romans 8 is the indwelling of the Holy Spirit, which is contrasted with the indwelling of sin in Romans 7 (vv. 17, 20). The indwelling Spirit does not keep us from having to struggle; neither does He always make us victors in the struggle so that we never give in to sin. Instead, the victory is in the fact that "there is therefore now no condemnation for those who are in Christ Jesus" (8:1). The struggle still takes place; sometimes we lose the struggle and sin. Yet we are victorious because, walking not after the flesh but after the Spirit, we are forgiven -- never condemned.

There are two stated qualifications characterizing the one for whom there is no condemnation: be "in Christ Jesus" (Romans 8:1) and "walk not according to the flesh but according to the Spirit" (v. 4). Paul was baptized into Christ as we should be (Acts 9:18; Galatians 3:27). "Walk not according to the flesh but according to the Spirit"

(Romans 8:4) describes Paul's mindset in Romans 7: "For I delight in the law of God, in my inner being" (v. 22); I "hate" the sin that I am doing (v. 15). When we meet the same two conditions, there is also no condemnation for us.

The same truth was taught in 1 John 1:7: "But if we walk in the light, as he is in the light, we have fellowship with one another, and the blood of Jesus his Son cleanses us from all sin." Although a child of God can sin so as to fall from the grace of God into eternal condemnation (Galatians 5:4), he does not fall from grace every time he sins. God does not count his sins against him (Romans 4:8). His sins are cleansed by the blood of Christ. Likewise, Christians – whose whole lives are aimed at heaven, who struggle with sin but hate it, who truly will to do and want to do as God directs – "by God's power are being guarded through faith for a salvation ready to be revealed in the last time" (1 Peter 1:5).

This is all in accord with a sentiment often ascribed to Restoration preacher Gus Nichols: "I believe in the possibility of apostasy, but I do not believe in the probability of apostasy." God does not wish for anyone to perish (2 Peter 3:9). In God's gracious providence, He is working to keep us saved and in the faith. He uses every resource, including His Spirit, to accomplish that. Thanks be to God through Jesus Christ our Lord.

The Leading of the Spirit

The Bible says the Holy Spirit leads the faithful Christian. "For all who are led by the Spirit of God are sons of God" (Romans 8:14). Or to put it a better way, faithful Christians follow the Spirit's leadership. But this discussion often leads to many questions among Christians. We will address a few of those here.

How Does the Holy Spirit Lead Us?

We can be certain the Holy Spirit leads us through Scripture. Peter spoke of "the Scripture ... which the Holy Spirit spoke beforehand by the mouth of David" (Acts 1:16), and he also said Scripture is produced by men who "spoke from God as they were carried along by the Holy Spirit" (2 Peter 1:21). So Scripture is the word of the Holy Spirit.

To the Thessalonian Christians, Paul said, "We also thank God constantly for this, that when you received the word of God, which you heard from us, you accepted it not as the word of men but as what it really is, the word of God, which is at work in you believers" (1 Thessalonians 2:13). And to the Corinthians, he wrote: "If anyone thinks that he is a prophet, or spiritual, he should acknowledge that the things I am writing to you are a command of the Lord. If anyone does not recognize this, he is not recognized" (1 Corinthians 14:37-38).

When the inspired words of apostles and prophets were originally heard, or when they are read in our time, it is a clear teaching of Scripture that they are words from God. When we obey what we read, we are being led by God and by His Spirit.

Certainly our relationship with the Holy Spirit (as well as with the Father and the Son) is a personal one; He is a person, and we are persons. He is, however, a Spirit person, not a flesh and blood person. Our relationship with Him, therefore, is not sensory – that is, it is not physically seen or felt. That does not make it impersonal. Scripture is a loving letter from a living God, and by reading it, we may personally commune with the divine Person whose word it is.

Does the Holy Spirit Also Lead Us in Other Ways?

Some say they hear an audible voice, but most of those who speak of being led directly by the Spirit rely on urges, impulses or strong inner convictions. There seem to be two major unaddressed questions regarding this view of the Spirit's leading.

(1) What is really being claimed?

Those who claim the Holy Spirit's direct leading almost always believe in the inspiration, authority and inerrancy of Scripture as well. They generally hasten to say, at least when asked, that their communication from the Spirit does not possess the same authority or assurance of truth as do the Scriptures. That is to their credit.

However, by the time the direct guidance of the Spirit is sufficiently hedged and explained so that every Christian is not deemed to be as inspired as the apostles, what is the Spirit supposed to have done? What value is there to a non-authoritative, possibly fallible impulse, and to what degree can or should it be attributed to God's Spirit?

Protestations to the contrary notwithstanding, these voices and impulses are often appealed to in order to convey the impression of divine authority. A church's minister is strongly convicted that his congregation needs to sell their present facility and move. He may say "God told me the church needs to move and rebuild" or at least maintain that he "feels led" in that decision. Obviously he intends to put God's authority behind the decision he is urging as best for his church.

Some in his congregation, however, may not be disposed to believe he is following God's direction. They may feel strongly that selling and moving is the wrong thing to do. In that case, one or more of them may say, "God told me we should stay where we are," or they may "feel led" to stay in the present facilities.

That introduces the second often unaddressed question.

(2) How can a person know when it is God's Spirit that he is hearing or feeling?

There are incidences of people believing God has told them to do something that is actually contrary to the will of God as revealed in Scripture. For instance, men and women who are married, but not to each other, have "fallen in love" and become convinced that God was telling them to leave their mates and remarry their new love. After all, few urges are stronger than that kind of urge, and it is easy for people to convince themselves that God wants them to be happy. Another example are parents who kill their children because a voice in their heads, which they claim to be God's, was telling them to do that.

Devout people who believe God communicates with them directly will quickly say they will not believe or follow any spirit or impulse that tells them to do something that violates Scripture. A question is nevertheless raised: If an impression that would otherwise be understood as the voice of God can give counsel contrary to the Bible, what assurance is there that the impression is God's word when it speaks on some matter not directly addressed by the Bible?

The lack of any criteria to distinguish the impulses that arise within ourselves because of our human desires – or that come, perhaps, from the devil – from those that are believed to come from God is a very serious problem. Many adherents in my experience refuse even to acknowledge the problem, much less try to suggest a reasonable criteria. Generally, the answer just becomes "You just know." But how is that different from the Mormon claim to "just know" by "the inner witness of the Spirit" that the Book of Mormon is true?

What Does the Bible Say?

Two types of Bible texts are used by advocates of the direct leading by the Spirit. Space will not allow the examination of all such texts, but we will look at one of each type.

(1) Scriptures specifically addressed to apostles and prophets, related to their special calling and inspiration.

A Scripture often cited in this category is John 16:13: "When the Spirit of truth comes, he will guide you into all the truth, for he will not speak on his own authority, but whatever he hears he will speak, and he will declare to you the things that are to come."

This is part of a long discourse of Jesus, which John was recording. Going all the way back to John 13, Jesus was with only His apostles and was talking to them. That fact alone would not show that today's disciples are not included in the promise, because Jesus said many things to the apostles that were to be passed on to later believers. All Bible believers, however, recognize that God did grant special powers to the apostles and early prophets and used them to reveal truths to subsequent generations. The text itself and its context, then – not the presuppositions we bring to the text – should determine whether this is a special promise to the apostles or a general promise to all disciples.

With this in mind, the scope of the promise in this verse becomes significant: "He will guide you into all the truth" (John 16:13). The apostles were given that promise and have now fulfilled its purpose, having written Scripture, which contains all the truth necessary for the man of God to "be complete, equipped for every good work" (2 Timothy 3:16-17). What believer today would really claim to be guided into all truth or to be kept from all error, as the apostles were?

Also note a parallel promise in the same discourse: "But the Helper, the Holy Spirit, whom the Father will send in my name, he will teach you all things and bring to your remembrance all that I have said to you" (John 14:26). This promise obviously applied only to those who had seen Jesus in the flesh and had personally heard Him say things that the Spirit would cause them to remember.

(2) Scriptures speaking of the Spirit's leading and guidance, though without specifying personal or inward guidance.

Scripture certainly states that we are to be led by the Spirit (cf. Romans 8:14), but those who read that as "inwardly led" or "led by impulses and urges" must bring those qualifiers and assumptions to the text; they do not get them from the text. Paul continued in the same context to say that the Spirit testifies and bears witness:

> For all who are led by the Spirit of God are sons of God. For you did not receive the spirit of slavery to fall back into fear, but you have received the Spirit of adoption as sons, by whom we cry, "Abba! Father!" The Spirit himself bears witness with our spirit that we are children of God, and if children, then heirs – heirs of God and fellow heirs with Christ, provided we suffer with him in order that we may also be glorified with him. (Romans 8:14-17)

How does the Spirit "bear witness"? The inspired author of Hebrews told us one way:

> And the Holy Spirit also bears witness to us; for after saying, "This is the covenant that I will make with them after those days, declares the Lord: I will put my laws on their hearts, and write them on their minds," then he adds, "I will remember their sins and their lawless deeds no more." (Hebrews 10:15-17)

The Holy Spirit witnesses, this text says, through the words of Scripture, specifically through Jeremiah 31:31 and 34, which are quoted in this text as His witness.

That the Spirit leads us and imparts revealed and inspired information to us through His inspired Scripture is certain. No information imparted by a vision, a voice or an impulse can be known to have come from the Spirit.

Assurance of Salvation

Likely, many people who have tried to lead someone away from religious error toward truth have had the experience of showing someone from Scripture that the inspired word of the Spirit makes baptism a requisite for salvation and received the response "But I know I'm saved. I feel it right here" (with a hand over the heart). Occasionally, the person may add a visual or auditory experience that he believes validates his feelings.

It is pointless to tell someone he did not feel, see or hear what he thinks he experienced. However, it is sometimes effective to help him see what his experience is telling him and contrast it with what Scripture says. People who really believe that Scripture is God's Word and who understand the truths of Scripture can sometimes be helped to see the stark contrast between what Scripture says and what their feelings say, and they may come to accept Scripture's testimony over their experience.

God and His Spirit are alive and active in the world. The Holy Spirit dwells in the faithful children of God as the guarantee of our inheritance until we acquire possession of it. God is King of kings and Lord of lords and rules in the affairs of men and nations. A sparrow cannot fall without His notice, and an empire cannot arise without His blessing. He works all things to the good of those who love Him.

God has not performed His last act of providence, but He has given His last revelation. Just as Christ was sacrificed "once for all" for the sins of the world (Hebrews 9:12), so the faith has been delivered "once for all" to the saints (Jude 3). God has offered His only atoning sacrifice and spoken His last word in Jesus Christ. Both the sacrifice and the revelation are sufficient. His once-for-all sacrifice serves as a propitiation "for the sins of the whole world" (1 John 2:2). His once-for-all Word, through the knowledge of Christ, supplies for us "all things that pertain to life and godliness" (2 Peter 1:3).

No religious view is more fraught with potential danger than one that equates one's personal impulses with a word from God. No life is more certainly pleasing to God and bound for eternal fellowship with Him than one that follows the leading of the Spirit through His revealed Word.

Questions

1. What must always supersede feelings in determining truth?

2. The first part of Philippians 2:12-13 – "Work out your own salvation with fear and trembling" – is often quoted with the second part left out. What does the second part say?

3. Paul prayed for the saints in Ephesus to be "strengthened with power" through what (cf. Ephesians 3:16)?

4. What is a purpose of God's Spirit dwelling in us according to 1 Corinthians 6?

5. What is the difference between committing a sin and living in sin?

6. What are the two stated conditions for being one for whom there is no condemnation?

7. How does the Holy Spirit lead us?

8. What criteria are available to help people decide whether someone who claims to be led in sensory ways is actually receiving messages from the Holy Spirit versus some other source?

9. How does the epistle to the Hebrews say the Holy Spirit witnesses to us?

10. Name two biblical concepts that were accomplished "once for all."

For Discussion

1. There are several theories concerning the Holy Spirit's indwelling, some of which deny He actually dwells in Christians at all. Discuss this in light of 1 Corinthians 6:19-20; Acts 5:32; and Ephesians 1:13-14.

2. Feelings do not prove something to be true; feelings result from what we believe on other grounds to be true. Elaborate on and/or illustrate that statement.

3. Describe Paul's (and our) struggle with sin (Romans 7).

4. Contrast the indwelling of sin (Romans 7:17, 20) and the indwelling of God's Spirit (8:9-11).

5. What are the dangers of believing that one's personal impulses are a word from God?

12

PROVIDENCE
and Angels

T he words translated "angel" in the Old and New Testaments – *malak*, Hebrew, and *aggelos*, Greek – primarily mean "messenger" and were frequently used of human messengers or ambassadors. There are, however, supernatural messengers – beings with a degree of divinity less than God, but greater than humans – and when the context indicates those beings are under consideration, translators use the word "angel."

For instance, as the children of Israel, under Moses' leadership, were going toward the land God had promised, God said, "Behold, I send an angel before you to guard you on the way and to bring you to the place that I have prepared" (Exodus 23:20). When Jesus was born, an angel appeared to shepherds near Bethlehem to announce to them the birth of "a Savior who is Christ the Lord" (Luke 2:9-11). Both God and the angels long for and rejoice at the repentance of sinners (15:7, 10). The question we must consider, then, is whether God continues to use angels as His agents as He providentially cares for His people.

Characteristics of Angels

Angels are spirit beings, not physical or fleshly. The writer of Hebrews called them "spirits" (Hebrews 1:14). After the resurrection – when

Christians will have immortal, imperishable and spiritual bodies (1 Corinthians 15:42-44) – we will be like the angels (Matthew 22:30), which includes not having the fleshly appetites upon which marriage is based.

Angels are invisible to mortal eyes and are only able to be seen at special appearances. Although frequently pictured in paintings and literature as females with wings, halos and harps, Jesus' words about them neither marrying nor giving in marriage (Matthew 22:30) suggest they may not possess gender. In their appearances, they often looked like ordinary people (Genesis 18; 19:1).

The cherubim and seraphim seen around the throne of God in prophetic visions are usually thought of as angelic beings, and they have wings – but many, not just two (Isaiah 6:2; Ezekiel 10:3-5). Angels who appeared and spoke are not said to have had wings. The halo was an invention of medieval artists to indicate divinity or saintliness; no one thinks angels really had them. Not angels but victorious saints in heaven have harps as they sing the song of Moses and the Lamb (Revelation 15:2-4).[1]

There are both good and bad angels. The angels who sinned, of which Peter and Jude wrote, are "kept in eternal chains under gloomy darkness until the judgment of the great day" (2 Peter 2:4; Jude 6). These are not the same as the angels who are involved on earth. However, the devil does have angels (Matthew 25:41), and they are likely the same as the demons or evil spirits that Jesus frequently encountered during His earthly ministry (Mark 7:25-26).

Paul said, "Satan disguises himself as an angel of light" (2 Corinthians 11:14). When Paul urged us to put on God's armor that we may be able to stand against the schemes of the devil, he added, "For we do not wrestle against flesh and blood, but against the rulers, against the authorities, against the cosmic powers over this present darkness, against the spiritual forces of evil in the heavenly places" (Ephesians 6:12).

During the personal ministry of Christ and His apostles, demons "possessed" people, possibly even against their will, but now neither Satan nor his angels have coercive power. They have schemes and they deceive. "When [Satan] lies, he speaks out of his own character, for he is a liar and the father of lies" (John 8:44). God evidently allowed demons to use miraculous powers and to possess people during the time of Christ on earth so that when Satan's powers and the powers of God's servants met, it would be obvious which were greater. As Jesus said, "But if it is by the Spirit of God that I cast out demons, then the kingdom of God has come upon you. Or how can someone enter a strong man's house and plunder his goods, unless he first binds the strong man? Then indeed he may plunder his house" (Matthew 12:28-29).

Angels, along with all other spiritual and supernatural beings, were created by God through Christ (Colossians 1:18; John 1:1). Because everything God created was good (Genesis 1:31) and some angels rebelled, a necessary conclusion seems to be that they, like humans, were created as freewill agents.

The angelic host seems to be ranked. There are archangels (1 Thessalonians 4:16). Michael, who is called an archangel (Jude 9), is also called "one of the chief princes" (Daniel 10:13). The thrones, dominions and powers noted in Ephesians 1:21 and Colossians 1:16 are thought to be various ranks of heavenly beings, or else they are thought to be invented as part of the "empty deceit" and "human tradition" Paul was opposing in the Colossian epistle (2:8).

The basic message of Colossians is that Christ has preeminence over everything – particularly over angels, demons, thrones, dominions, etc., because He made them. If the saints in Colossae were disturbed at the thought of having to keep all those mysterious spiritual beings pacified, Paul's message was "Don't worry about them; Christ made them and is over them. Get right with Christ, and He will take care of them." The same message applies today with any superstitions one might have of broken mirrors or black cats.

Do We Have Guardian Angels?

Many believe every child and every Christian have a personal guardian angel. A popular painting by Heilige Schutzengel shows a female angel hovering protectively above a young girl and boy as they cross a rickety wooden bridge. A print of this picture hangs in many homes. As the idea of guardian angels is usually conceived, every child of God is supposed to have an angel assigned to him or her, who is always present although invisible and who provides protection from various kinds of temptation, evil and harm.

The subject of guardian angels has been a matter of long-standing disagreement among men we all likely honor as scholarly and wise. When Peter, after being miraculously freed from jail, appeared at the front door of the house where the believers were gathered, their first thought was "It is his angel" (Acts 12:15). J.W. McGarvey said this thought was "based on the supposition that every man has an angel, which is a true Scriptural idea." [2] However, David Lipscomb said: "The idea of guardian angels is attended with some evil; it is best not to teach it." [3]

Some passages in the Bible give rise to the idea of individual guardian angels. The devil, in tempting Jesus, "took him to the holy city and set him on the pinnacle of the temple and said to him, 'If you are the Son of God, throw yourself down' " (Matthew 4:5-6). Then he quoted Psalm 91:11-12: " 'He will command his angels concerning you,' and 'On their hands they will bear you up, lest you strike your foot against a stone' " (Matthew 4:6). Jesus resisted the temptation on the grounds that God's promises are not to be deliberately tested, but the psalm does imply that angels are at least sometimes involved in God's watchful care over His faithful ones.

In the chapter that begins with Jesus telling His disciples they must "become like children" if they are to enter the kingdom (Matthew 18:1-4), Jesus warned: "See that you do not despise one of these little ones. For I tell you that in heaven their angels always see the face of my Father who is in heaven" (v. 10). Whatever else may be said about who "these little ones" are or about the work of "their angels," this passage does not say anything about any activity of angels on earth; rather, it affirms activity in heaven.

Of course, what God and His angels do in heaven can affect what happens on earth. Hebrews 1 – which primarily shows that Jesus, as the Son of God, is far superior to the angels – concludes with these words: "Are [angels] not all ministering spirits sent out to serve for the sake of those who are to inherit salvation?" (v. 14).

The basic questions raised by those who doubt the doctrine of guardian angels also must be raised regarding any idea of providence. A Christian falls over a cliff and receives a broken arm and leg and various painful contusions when he might well have broken his neck and been paralyzed or killed. Someone says, "See, his guardian angel was with him." Is it not all right if we wonder why his angel did not keep him from falling over the cliff at all? And what about the faithful Christian who is killed in an untimely accident? What happened to his guardian angel?

It is a fact to be considered – and that must be factored in as an integral part of whatever doctrine about providence one believes – that neither a guardian angel nor God Himself will always keep calamities from happening to faithful Christians. Whatever terrible thing does happen, though, God does care, and He will provide so that some good will result from it. Faithful Christians suffer and even die – sometimes horribly, sometimes prematurely – but victory is still assured. Death is followed by resurrection. Suffering brings glory (Romans 8:18).

There is at least one beautiful service we are told angels render for saints. When Lazarus died at the rich man's gate, "he was carried by the angels to Abraham's side" (Luke 16:22). That thought has brought comfort to many dying saints as well as to their loved ones.

Agents of God and His Word

Whatever else angels may do, they have served as God's agents in communicating His word to His people, as the Hebrews writer explained: "Therefore we must pay much closer attention to what we have heard, lest we drift away from it. For since the message declared by angels proved to be reliable ... how shall we escape if we neglect such a great salvation?" (Hebrews 2:1-3). A major point of Hebrews 1–2 is that Christ, who brings God's word in "these last days" (1:2), is far superior to the angels who helped bring God's word "long ago" (v. 1).

Paul and Stephen also testified to the work of angels as conveyors of God's word. Paul said: "Why then the law? It was added because of transgressions, until the offspring should come to whom the promise had been made, and it was put in place through angels by an intermediary" (Galatians 3:19). Stephen said, "You ... received the law as delivered by angels and did not keep it" (Acts 7:53).

Along with assisting in delivering God's word, angels often acted on behalf of God in biblically recorded miraculous events. When Daniel was thrown into the lions' den and the next morning was unharmed, "Daniel said to the king, 'O king, live forever! My God sent his angel and shut the lions' mouths, and they have not harmed me' " (Daniel 6:21-22). When Sennacherib's Assyrian army was approaching Jerusalem to defeat and destroy it, the godly King Hezekiah prayed, and God's prophet Isaiah assured him:

> "Therefore thus says the LORD concerning the king of Assyria: He shall not come into this city or shoot an arrow there, or come before it with a shield or cast up a siege mound against it. By the way that he came, by the same he shall return, and he shall not come into this city, declares the LORD. For I will defend this city to save it, for my own sake and for the sake of my servant David." And that night the angel of the LORD went out and struck down 185,000 in the camp of the Assyrians. And when people arose early in the morning, behold, these were all dead bodies. (2 Kings 19:32-35)

The Bible teaches that God cares for us, that He providentially intervenes for us, and that He has sometimes used angels to accomplish that. We can know, therefore, by faith that He does such things. What we cannot know is whether He has done so in a specific instance. Miracles are signs and clearly identifiable, obviously done by God's power. God's providence, whether effected by angels or not, is "perhaps."

Questions

1. What are angels?

2. Describe a few characteristics of angels.

3. Were angels active in the Old Testament, the New Testament, or both?

4. After death, will Christians be angels or like the angels?

5. Does Satan have angels?

6. Where did angels come from?

7. What was always the result when demonic powers and the powers of Jesus Christ were in conflict?

8. Who did Paul and Stephen say delivered the law?

9. Who did God use to communicate the New Testament message to humanity? Which book of the Bible discusses His greatness over the angels?

10. Have angels ever been used by God to protect His people?

For Discussion

1. Do you think every Christian has a guardian angel? What scriptural support can you provide for your reasoning?

2. What kinds of questions are legitimately raised about the concept of guardian angels? How are those questions equally relevant to the discussion of providence, whether or not angels are involved?

13

PROVIDENCE
and Salvation

God's intentional will for all mankind is our salvation (1 Timothy 2:4). Since mankind's sin, He has still worked to that end. His providence may be seen in the circumstances of Christ's coming into the world, in helping those who hunger and thirst for righteousness to be satisfied, and in opening doors of opportunity for the gospel to be preached.

The Fullness of Time

When God sent His Son to redeem mankind, it was, by God's gracious providence, just at the right time and with all the just right circumstances in place. "The fullness of time had come" (Galatians 4:4).

God's providential use of Nebuchadnezzar and the Babylonians to punish His people forever cured the Jews of idolatry. The forced exile of the best of the Jews to pagan Babylon produced a chastened and renewed remnant through which God was able to fulfill His promises concerning His coming kingdom and Messiah (cf. Jeremiah 24). Although some Jews continued in apathy, neglect of the poor, sexual immorality, extortion and vain worship and although most Jews rebelled in unbelief against the Messiah whom God had sent to them (John 1:11), they never again turned to idols or other gods.

Also as a result of the Babylonian conquest — and, thus, forced separation from the temple — the Jews developed the synagogue and its teaching and worship styles. Paul and other Christian missionaries used the synagogues very effectively in cities all across the Roman Empire for spreading the gospel.

Many years before Paul, but after the Medes and Persians were used by God to conquer and punish Babylon for its atrocities and violence (Isaiah 13:17-19), Alexander the Great, of Greece, conquered the Persian Empire and became ruler of the known world of his day. He did so out of an evangelistic zeal, believing the world would be greatly improved if people were forced to adopt Greek language, culture, art and philosophy. As a result of his conquests, Greek became virtually a universal language, spoken and understood in every country alongside its native language. That fact also contributed to relative ease in the spread of the gospel.

Some 600 years before Christ, God was developing and revealing His plan, making it known through visions shown to Nebuchadnezzar and interpreted by the prophet Daniel. He revealed that God would send His Messiah and establish His kingdom during the reign of the Roman emperors, who had conquered the heirs of Alexander (Daniel 2:44). *Pax Romana*, the peace enforced by Roman legions and the system of roads built by the Romans ("All roads lead to Rome") made travel throughout the empire safer and more convenient than at any previous time in history.

Many devout God-fearers, Gentiles attracted to Jewish monotheism and the high moral character of the God of the Jews, were loosely but admiringly attached to the Jewish synagogues throughout the Roman Empire. They provided a large pool of potential converts to apostolic preaching.

Truly, providentially, it was the right time for Christ to be born and for the gospel to be spread throughout the world in one generation (Colossians 1:6, 23).

Honest Seekers Find

People often ask, "If Jesus really is the resurrected Son of God" or "If baptism really is essential to salvation," etc., "then why are there so many intelligent people even with doctoral degrees who can't see it?" The answer to that kind of question is clear. It is not IQ or educational attainment that determines whether a person will understand and submit to God's will when it is presented.

Jesus said, "Blessed are the poor in spirit, for theirs is the kingdom of heaven" (Matthew 5:3); "Blessed are those who hunger and thirst for righteousness, for they shall be satisfied" (v. 6); and "If anyone's will is to do God's will, he will know whether the teaching is from God or whether I am speaking on my own authority" (John 7:17). These promises imply that people who know they are not smart enough or good enough to save themselves (the "poor in spirit"), people who hungrily desire to be righteous before God, and people who genuinely want to do what God commands them to do are the ones who will recognize and obey the truth when they hear it.

These promises seem to imply further that honest seekers will somehow have opportunities to be exposed to the saving gospel truth, an implication that takes us again to the providence of God. One example of this occurs in Acts 8, when Philip encountered an Ethiopian eunuch on the road to Gaza. This eunuch was the treasurer in the court of Queen Candace and had traveled about 200 miles to the temple in Jerusalem to worship. As he returned to Ethiopia, he was reading the prophet Isaiah, likely on a scroll. Scrolls were not common possessions. The unnamed treasurer had likely invested a considerable sum to own one, and as he traveled, he was reading and pondering what he read. All of that would seem to indicate he was hungering and thirsting for righteousness.

Philip, who possessed and used miraculous spiritual gifts (Acts 8:6-7), was visited by an angel, who told him to leave the very successful gospel meeting in Samaria in which he was engaged and to "go toward the south to the road that goes down from Jerusalem to Gaza" (v. 26). This was a long journey on foot, but God's timing was perfect. Just as Philip arrived at that road, the treasurer's chariot, coming from Jerusalem, was in sight. The Spirit then spoke to Philip: "Go over and join this chariot" (v. 29). Perhaps more than coincidentally, the treasurer, at that moment, was reading the very part of the scroll (Isaiah 53 as we designate it today) that spoke so clearly of the Messiah's suffering and death as atonement for our sins.

God always uses human beings – never angels or the Holy Spirit or a voice out of the heavens – to speak the gospel to those who need to hear it. The "treasure" of the gospel resides not in heavenly messengers but in "jars of clay" or human beings (2 Corinthians 4:7). Miracles were involved in this instance of the eunuch's conversion, as the angel and the Spirit spoke directly to Philip. Evidently providence was also involved, as Philip and the eunuch arrived at the same place at the same time as the eunuch was reading the very verses prophesying Jesus' work as the Messiah. Philip, the evangelist, began at that scripture and preached Jesus. The Ethiopian eunuch was converted and baptized, and he went on his way rejoicing because of his salvation. He had hungered after righteousness, and through the providence and grace and gospel of God, he was satisfied.

God miraculously and directly led Paul and his co-workers – Silas, Timothy and Luke – to Macedonia to preach. Taking a ship from Troas, they "made a direct voyage to Samothrace," an island off the coast of Macedonia, "and the following day to Neapolis, and from there to Philippi" (Acts 16:11-12). Literally, they ran a straight course (Greek: *euthudromesamen*) to Samothrace. Typically, unless the wind is blowing precisely in the direction they wish to go, sailors have to "tack" – that is, they have to set the sails so as to go diagonally, first one way and then another, in order to make progress in the general direction they wish to go. That Paul and his companions ran a straight course means they went quickly because they had a favorable wind. Providence? Perhaps.

An earnest seeker is promised he will find the truth. What if, by God's providence, the seeker is brought in contact with you or me? How important does that make it for us to take advantage of every opportunity to speak the truth to honest seekers who come our way?

Providence Opens Doors

Paul spoke of open doors of opportunity. He told the Corinthian church of his plans to work for a considerable time in Ephesus "for a wide door for effective work has opened to me, and there are many adversaries" (1 Corinthians 16:9). He did not say, "I have opened a door." It was opened by another – in this case, undoubtedly by God. Providence worked toward the conversion of some in Ephesus whose will it was to do God's will. An open door, however, does not mean the absence of obstacles or opposition.

When Paul and Barnabas returned to Antioch after completing their first missionary journey, they reported to the church, telling "all that God had done with them, and how he had opened a door of faith to the Gentiles" (Acts 14:27). They had great success on that first missionary journey, establishing churches and appointing elders on the island of Cyprus and in Antioch of Pisidia, Iconium, Lystra and Derbe. They attributed their success to God opening the door. That is providence.

As one who sought to preach in large metropolitan centers where no apostle had gone, it is not surprising that Paul had his heart set on preaching in Rome (cf. Romans 1:15). However, later in his epistle to the Romans, he said he had been laboring "from Jerusalem and all the way around to Illyricum" (v. 19), preaching the gospel where other apostles and preachers had not been. "This is the reason why I have so often been hindered from coming to you," Paul explained (15:22). He had been hindered by his personal decision to work elsewhere first. Providence opens doors, but it does not dictate or coerce.

Paul wanted to go to Rome, but God had also planned for Paul to preach in Rome. As Paul was dealing with a gang of Jews in Jerusalem who had vowed to kill him, the Lord stood by him one night and said, "Take courage, for as you have testified to the facts about me in Jerusalem, so you must testify also in Rome" (Acts 23:11). Paul probably thought he would go to Rome as a missionary, just as he had gone to Galatia, Ephesus, Macedonia and Achaia. Instead, he went to Rome as a prisoner of Caesar, indicted by the Jews for preaching the gospel to the Gentiles.

Still under the protection and help of God's providential care, however, he was allowed to live in his house and to receive any visitors who came to see him. While in Rome, he asked the Colossians to pray that he would have opportunities to make the gospel known. "At the same time, pray also for us, that God may open to us a door for the word, to declare the mystery of Christ, on account of which I am in prison" (Colossians 4:3). Thus, he continued to preach the gospel to the people of Rome.

Although he had the freedom to receive visitors, he was not free. He was likely chained day and night to a succession of Roman soldiers (Acts 28:16; Colossians 4:18). As Caesar's prisoner, he was guarded by Caesar's imperial guard. In Acts 12:3-4, four squads of soldiers were assigned to Peter to be sure he did not escape. Assuming similar arrangements were made for Paul, 16 soldiers would circulate in and out of his house, one or two always being chained to Paul. Paul, therefore, had a built-in captive audience. One might wonder, "Who was really the prisoner?" He wrote, therefore,

> I want you to know, brothers, that what has happened to me has really served to advance the gospel, so that it has become known throughout the whole imperial guard and to all the rest that my imprisonment is for Christ. (Philippians 1:12-13)

Through God's providence, Paul's imprisonment, an apparently bad thing, resulted in the conversion of some of his guards and even some others in Caesar's household (Philippians 4:22) – a good thing. Thus, we have another example confirming God's promise in Romans 8:28: "And we know that for those who love God all things work together for good, for those who are called according to his purpose."

Sometimes extraneous circumstances hindered even an apostle from taking advantage of an open door. "When I came to Troas to preach the gospel of Christ, even though a door was opened for me in the Lord, my spirit was not at rest because I did not find my brother Titus there. So I took leave of them and went on to Macedonia" (2 Corinthians 2:12-13). Paul was simply not emotionally prepared to take advantage of the opportunity to preach at Troas. Providence opens doors of opportunity, but it does not force us to walk through them.

In Jesus Christ's letters to the seven churches of Asia, He said to the church in Philadelphia, "The words of the holy one, the true one, who has the key of David, who opens and no one will shut, who shuts and no one opens" (Revelation 3:7). Emphasis here is on the sovereignty of Christ. No one can open what He has shut; no one can shut what He has opened. Jesus maintains an open door to salvation for everyone. He said: "Behold, I stand at the door and knock. If anyone hears my voice and opens the door, I will come in to him and eat with him, and he with me" (v. 20). The door to redemption is open, and everyone is invited.

Conclusion

It is God's intentional will that every person He created in His image be saved. "The Lord is not slow to fulfill his promise as some count slowness, but is patient toward you, not wishing that any should perish, but that all should reach repentance" (2 Peter 3:9). "This is good, and it is pleasing in the sight of God our Savior, who desires all people to be saved and to come to the knowledge of the truth" (1 Timothy 2:3-4). Still, God does not force or coerce. He has graciously given His Son for our redemption. He often provides opportunities for the sincere seeker to hear. Yet the final choice is ours.

God is always good, He always cares, and He always provides what is good for His faithful children. But He does so according to His definition of good – not ours. He provides according to His timetable – not ours. His blessings reach all the way into eternity.

Though I, thro' the valley of shadow,
O'er mountain or troubled sea,
And oft in the darkness, have travelled,
The Lord has been mindful of me!

Much more than my grief and my sorrow,
Much more than adversity,
Much more than the all I have given,
The Lord has been mindful of me!

I'm rich! I am saved! I am happy!
I've health and prosperity!
I've friends! I have doors ever open!
The Lord has been mindful of me!

The Lord has been mindful of me!
He blesses and blesses again!
My God is the God of the living!
How excellent is His name!

– "The Lord Has Been Mindful of Me"
L.O. Sanderson, 1948

Questions

1. Describe some of the circumstances that made the timing of Christ's coming to the earth opportune.

2. Why do some people receive and obey the gospel when they hear it while others reject it?

3. Who does God always use to convey the gospel to those who need to hear it?

4. What does it mean to say "God opens doors"?

5. Paul told the Philippians that his imprisonment in Rome had worked out for the furtherance of the gospel. How was that true?

6. If God opens a door, do we have to go through it? If we do not go through it, do we sin?

7. Christ has the key to what door, which is always open?

For Discussion

1. Illustrate the principle that those who hunger and thirst for righteousness will be filled, using the biblical story of Philip and the Ethiopian eunuch.

2. What responsibility is put on us by the realization that God may providentially bring a hungering seeker into contact with us as people who know the gospel?

Endnotes

Chapter 3

1 Leslie D. Weatherhead, *The Will of God* (Nashville: Abingdon-Cokesbury, 1944). Although his will of God categories resonate biblically, he expresses views about the cross and mankind's fall into sin that are not biblical.

Chapter 4

1 J.W. McGarvey and Philip Y. Pendleton, *Standard Bible Commentary: Thessalonians, Corinthians, Galatians, Romans* (Cincinnati: Standard, 1916) 365.

Chapter 8

1 The Nuzi tablets, named for the Mesopotamian city of Nuzi where they were found, were excavated between 1925 and 1931 by the American School of Oriental Research. About 20,000 small clay tablets of cuneiform writing revealed customs and mores of life in the second and third millenniums B.C. Many of them shed light on the social customs of the biblical patriarchal era.

Chapter 10

1 Tertullian, *Apologeticus* 50.

2 Because Stephen (Acts 7:54-60) and James (12:1-2) of the Jerusalem church had suffered death, this verse may have had a bearing on the intended audience for the Hebrews epistle. That discussion is not germane, however, to the subject of this book.

Chapter 12

1 It is unlikely that harps, gates of pearl, or a golden street are literal (Revelation 15:2-4; 21:21). We will have "spiritual" bodies (1 Corinthians 15:44). The rest of 1 Corinthians 15:35-50 implies that material things may be analogous to heaven's beauty, but gold and pearls would have no actual value there.

2 J.W. McGarvey, *New Commentary on Acts of the Apostles,* reprint (Cincinnati: Standard, n.d.) 237.

3 David Lipscomb in H. Leo Boles, *A Commentary on the Gospel According to Matthew* (Nashville: Gospel Advocate, 1952) 373.

About the Author

Cecil May Jr. was appointed dean emeritus of the V.P. Black College of Biblical Studies at Faulkner University in Montgomery, Ala., on June 1, 2013. Prior to that, May served as dean of the college for 15 years, and prior to working at Faulkner, he served as president of Magnolia Bible College in Mississippi for more than 17 years. He was appointed "Distinguished Professor" by the board of trustees at MBC, and the classroom building was named in his honor.

May received his B.A., M.A. and M.Div. degress from Harding University. He was also awarded an honorary LL.D. degree by Freed-Hardeman University. May began preaching as a student at Harding in 1951 and spent his early years preaching primarily in the Mississippi area, specifically in Holly Springs, Ripley, Ashland, Fulton and Vicksburg. He also served for two years on the Bible faculty of Columbia Christian College in Portland, Ore., and for three-and-a-half years as dean and a Bible teacher at Heritage Christian University. May continues to preach and lecture extensively, as well as write for several publications. He has been writing the back page column for the *Gospel Advocate*, titled "Finally, Brethren," since July 2012.

In 2003, May and his wife, Winnie, received Harding's Distinguished Christian Service Award, and in 2008, the Cloverdale Center for Family Strengths presented them with the "Tower of Strength" Family Award. In 2012, Mr. and Mrs. Harrell Freeman established the Cecil and Winnie May Endowed Chair of Biblical Studies at Faulkner in their honor.

The Mays have four children and five grandchildren. Both of their sons and one son-in-law are preachers.

CPSIA information can be obtained at www.ICGtesting.com
Printed in the USA
LVOW12s0525150814

399273LV00004B/4/P